# The Relevance of Philosophy

Edited by

Professor Sylvanus Ifeanyichukwu Nnoruka

DORRANCE PUBLISHING CO

EST. 1920

PITTSBURGH, PENNSYLVANIA 15238

Dorrance Publishing Co
585 Alpha Drive
Pittsburgh, PA 15238
Visit our website at *www.dorrancebookstore.com*

ISBN: 978-1-6366-1455-7
eISBN: 978-1-6366-1641-4

# INTRODUCTION

How relevant is philosophy to life, precisely human life? This can be regarded as a perennial question. The basic question that gave rise to pre-Socratic philosophy – *ex qua materia constituiti mundi* – (of what material is this world made of? Or what is the primary source or cause or origin [*arch* ] of everything?) could be regarded as the first attempt to answer this question. The various responses given by the presocratic philosophers, Thales – water, Anaximander – indeterminate boundless (*Apeiron*), Anaximenes – air are generally regarded as the beginning of the enterprise of philosophy. "Anaximenes names two processes through which things come to be and perish: condensation and rarefaction. They are explained by the fact that air is in constant motion." To be noted is "the attempt at explaining all appearances with the quantitative concept of varying density. In this respect Anaximenes is a precursor of modern science."[1] These responses mark the emergence of philosophy from Greek mythology. Medieval philosophy on its part offered an answer by way of proposing rational answers to the problems posed by the Christian faith. Thus, medieval philosophy also known as Christian philosophy is the use made of philosophical notions by Christian writers of the time. Such was the young Justin the Martyr's notion of philosophy. Precisely, that the primary task of a philosopher is to investigate the deity.[2] Other examples are the five proofs or ways of demonstrating the existence of God (*Quinque viae*) of Thomas Aquinas. They are proofs from: motion, efficient cause, necessary versus possible

---

[1] Fiedo Ricken, *Philosophy of the Ancients*, University of Notre Dame Press, Indiana, 1991, 16-17.

[2] Etienne Gilson, *History of Christian Philosophy in the Middle Ages*, Sheed and Ward Press, London, 1980, 11.

being, the degrees of perfection, order of the universe. There is also Anselm who (like Augustine) wanted to employ reason to understand what he was believing. His method was *faith seeking understanding* (*Fides Querens Intellectum*).

Descartes inaugurated a new and unprecedented era by drawing attention sorely to the Thinking being; that is, emphasis on the first person singular (*Cogito Ergo sum*). Following the renaissance philosophy that cleared the ground for him, his philosophy was man-centred. This makes the problem still more complicated. Man's capacity to know was taken for granted. Kant took an unprecedented step through his critical philosophy. He took a step higher than Descartes by posing the question: Can the human mind know, and if the human mind can know, what can the human mind know? He makes his point clearer by posing three questions concerning the 'I' – what can I know? what can I do? what can I hope for? Though more critical than Descartes, nevertheless, the 'I' still dominates. Hegel stretched this line of thought to an unprecedented and clearly unacceptable height through his idealism. At this point the answer to the question we originally posed, that is, whether philosophy is relevant to life is clearly answered in the negative. That is, many were regrettably convinced that philosophy has no relevance to day-to-day life.

However, with the dawn of the 20th century, there was a turning point. Is philosophy simply an idealistic exercise or is there a way of conducting the exercise of philosophy so that it has relevance to life? Many thinkers answered not only in the affirmative, but they also initiated modes of philosophizing to concretise the affirmation. Existentialism stands out foremost. It focussed on the uniqueness of each human individual as distinguished from abstract universal human qualities. Also, a critical and practical attempt to bring a logical conclusion to the perennial and 'bloody' war among philosophers on the question: what is truth? gave birth to two modes of arriving at the truth – phenomenology and hermeneutics. With regard to the former, the important slogan is: *Zu den Sachen Selbst* (i.e., back to the things themselves). It means back to the things themselves "as the 'objectifying' constructions of our conceptual judgements"; to the phenomena themselves as opposed to concepts and other derivatives from immediate experience. The aim of phenomenology is "to demonstrate how the world is an experience which we live before it becomes an object which we know in some impersonal or detached fashion."[3] The high point of Edmund Husserl's epochal contribution here is the Intentionality. That is that the world derives its meaning in and through consciousness. It is disclosed as a world that is always for consciousness. And consciousness is always consciousness of something. It is consciousness of something other than itself. It is consciousness of the world. Also, hermeneutics is an attempt to overcome methods, to dispense with overemphasis on proofs and arguments and the quest for certainty and emphasize instead the shared understandings that we already have with one another. The substance of philosophy becomes dialogue rather than individual phenomenology or abstract proofs. This is the main point developed by Hans Georg Gadamer in his work, *Truth and Method*.

The result is that today, it has become a truism that philosophy is relevant to the lifeworld. Philosophy becomes a torch which when flashed through critical thinking sheds light on how to salvage man in the lifeworld from the dungeon of intellectual and social darkness to light.

This book is a manifestation of the possibility of the relevance of philosophy. The context is the nagging and unfortunately political malaise in Nigeria, west Africa. It celebrated its sixtieth Independence anniversary on 1 October 2020. Since the Independence, it seems most of the time to be hanging on a balance. It is still unfortunately in search of a social and political direction. Philosophy lecturers of the Department of Philosophy, Bigard Memorial Seminary, Enugu believe that there is still hope. Pragmatically, this group devoted its Monthly Lecture of the year, 2019 to the mode of realization of the hope.

Fabian Ikechukwu Agudosi, writing on "African Communalism and the Quest for Sustainable Development in Africa" opines that it is still a worrisome issue that despite so many conferences, seminars, workshops, etc. held in a bid to bring about sustainable development in Africa, such efforts have not yielded the expected results. That is why his paper is an attempt to view and review how sustainable development can be attained for the benefit of the African peoples. Many scholars have equally proffered varied solutions that will make sustainable development *a fait accompli*, but some of these solutions have been

---

[3] R. Kearney, *Modern Movements in European Philosophy*, Manchester University Press, 1986,13.

vitiated in their methods and/or operations because they are not rooted in our culture. He, therefore, advocates that proper adherence to, and adoption of African communalism will be profitable in bringing about sustainable development in Africa.

Kevin Udewagu in his paper, "Democracy and Freedom: Towards a Redefinition of Nigerian Democracy" addresses the problem of democracy in Nigeria. Given the apparent weakness of our democratic regimes, past and present, evident in a total system collapse, the paper points out part of the problems with suggestive measures. Democracy well understood and adapted within a political community, questions the place of the people within the confines of its application. However, our wrong interpretation of democracy is based on a misunderstanding of the principle of freedom on which democratic principles stand. The consequence is enormous – a democracy at crossroads. Military intervention in Nigerian politics contributes greatly to the menace. As a way out, this paper suggests constitutional restructuring. This will not only afford the people an opportunity of saying their mind in matters concerning the affairs of their political society but will also address the lopsided sense of justice which according to Aristotle, is a trigger of revolution.

Writing on "The Centralized Federalism in Nigerian Political Structure: A Critical Analysis for Decentralization" Eugene C. Anowai and Steven Chukwujekwu observe that Nigeria is a multiethnic, multinational, multi-religious, multicultural country characterized by deep-rooted ethnic diversities and political heterogeneities. It began to adopt a federal system from October 1954 to properly accommodate the heterogeneities and pluralities among the regions. The federal system has been in operation since then. But this federal system is not working and creates complex challenges, due to the diverse nature of Nigeria and the centralized nature of its federalism. Therefore, it is opined that for it to work properly as a true federation, it is imperative that it must be decentralized. So rather than 'one size fits all', nature of Nigerian federalism, this paper argues that devolved government bodies will tailor public services and regulations more efficiently and flexibly to meet the needs of each region.

On the topic "Money Politics in Nigeria", Cletus Umezinwa argues that the bane of Nigeria's failure is money politics. The solution lies in putting in place a political arrangement that would prevent people from enriching themselves from public trust. He suggests that a way to increase the number of people in the middle class is to empower the citizens financially with grants to finance their education and lend them money to begin their private businesses, a policy which, if properly executed, can lead to less importation of certain products and encourage the exportation of others. For government to have sufficient resources to fulfil its obligation, there is need to have appropriate tax regime, have other sources of income apart from oil and then close conduit pipes through which country's money get into private pockets. The middle class must be empowered. Cletus Umezinwa proposes national dialogue.

In her paper, "Revolution of Minds in the Nigeria Project: The Socratic Paradigm" Nkechi Ezeanyino proposes a Nigerian philosophy of education. It is a process of the reorientation of the mentality of the young Nigerians. To that effect, she suggests the use of Socratic Method to groom from the grassroots our young minds to right thinking, right understanding and right conduct. Teachers must be groomed in this method. She suggests the inclusion of Socrates and the Socratic Method in the Curriculum of our Teacher Education. This should be made compulsory subject and not elective. Then follows the Citizenship or Civic Education, the education aimed at building morally sound and upright citizens who would ensure the promotion of political and socio-economic development of Nigeria. This education must start from Nursery, through Primary, Secondary and Tertiary levels. If the mentality of the future generation is re-orientated or reformed, it is her submission that hope will be rekindled for our Nation.

In the "Cultural Relevance of Education", Sylvanus Ifeanyichukwu Nnoruka maintains that every individual has the innate capacity of being educated. Authentic education incorporates the basic aspects of human formation: physical, mental, moral. While recognizing the relevance of the known theories of education and taking Africa and precisely the Igbo cultural group as our case study, with the illumination of the hermeneutical method, he argues and asserts that for any educational system to correctly and positively influence the individual, it must be relevant to his/her environment; it must recognize the *who* of the individual. The individual thus educated is a balanced person who also recognizes the relevance of the other. It is only thus that education can contribute to the fulfillment and happiness of the individual, the peace and development of the environment and the entire humanity.

According to Humphrey Uche Ani, the problem with Nigeria is not about laws and rules, but about people who should have the duty and good will to put them into practice. Best laws make no meaning when not applied. And the best national visions will have no effect and impact if they are not expressed in action and practical development. Therefore, his paper "The Law of Emergent Probability and National Development" looks at the problem of Nigeria as coming from the wrong development of the Nigerian personality before looking at the social impacts of such wrong development in the national development project. It is a kind of down-to-top approach to the Nigerian national development project, using what Bernard Lonergan called the law of emergent probability. The submission of this paper, therefore, is that the task of national development in Nigeria must start in the formation and development of the individual Nigerians.

Writing on the topic, "The Modern Sophists in Religious Garb: The Nigerian Experience", Modestus Anyaegbu insists that one of the major reasons why Pentecostalism and their false messages of hope attract and keep attracting many poor people is the lack of basic and proper education. Some Pastors in this country are quacks who are into the industry simply to make money. Inability of the government to reasonably create job opportunity contributes to the growth of the Pentecostal Industry. A way out could be the addition of Socrates' notion of moral goodness in the educational curriculum. The notion emphasizes that the first and chief concern for everyone is not for your bodies nor for your possessions, but for the highest welfare of your souls. An additional solution for this religious menace in Nigeria would be to establish stricter rules and enforce them. But can corruption ever allow such rules to work in Nigeria?

Chrysanthus Nnaemeka Ogbozor argues in his paper, "The Transcendental Primordial Values of the Human Society vis-à-vis the Nigerian State" that though a state may have begun spontaneously in a natural way as Aristotle once described, still the state cannot endure or survive as a social institution unless it is founded on some primordial values that have transcendental outlook. Such survival, many have speculated, seems to be eluding Nigeria amid unprecedented phenomena being witnessed in the society today. In the light of the foregoing, this paper proposes an end to "paper/certificate education" and a strong pursuit of cognitive and volitional education. The former is a continuous effort to know and to be able to rationally sort out values in the descending order of primordiality; the latter is the praxis of acting in accordance with the hierarchically arranged values. For nothing gets done, except by doing it. The act of doing is primarily the movement of the will – voluntas – and hence, the education and re-education of the will must complement the knowledge of values. This paper is, therefore, ethically and metaphysically oriented.

I recommend this book to all Nigerians and indeed every African. It is not enough to keep bemoaning the unfortunate and regrettable events of the past – slavery, colonialism, military intervention in politics – that have crippled the development of our country/continent. We now have the mantle of leadership. Let us prove to the world that through our originality generated by critical reasoning, we can successfully generate unique solutions to our problems. These solutions must *ab initio* come from us. Others are there only to help us. We must show the determination to succeed before they can help us correctly. This book challenges us to original thinking.

We sincerely thank all the contributors for the time and pains taken to write the articles. They thereby urge others not to lose hope. That through our hard work and originality, we can take Africa to enviable social and political haven. We also thank the other lecturers of the Philosophy Department for their critical contributions during our delivery sessions. We are grateful to the Rector of the Seminary, Very Rev. Father Dr. Albert Ikpenwa for creating a conducive environment that has made this book possible. To all the others, we say a big THANK YOU.


Sylvanus Ifeanyichukwu Nnoruka

# NOTES ON CONTRIBUTORS

**Barrister Fabian Ikechukwu Agudosi** is a lecturer in the Department of Philosophy, Faculty of Arts, Chukwuemeka Odumegwu Ojukwu University, Igbariam Campus, Nigeria.

**Rev. Father Kevin Udenwagu**, Ph.D. teaches Philosophy in Bigard Memorial Seminary, Enugu, Nigeria.

**Rev. Father Eugene C. Anowai,** Professor, teaches Philosophy in the Department of Philosophy, Faculty of Arts, Chukwuemeka Odumegwu Ojukwu University, Igbariam Campus, Nigeria.

**Rev. Father Stephen Chukwujekwu,** Professor, teaches Philosophy in the Department of Philosophy, Faculty of Arts, Chukwuemeka Odumegwu Ojukwu University, Igbariam Campus, Nigeria.

**Rev. Father Cletus Umezinwa**, Associate Professor, teaches Philosophy in Bigard Memorial Seminary, Enugu, Nigeria.

**Sr. Nkechi Ezeanyino**, DDL, Ph.D. teaches Philosophy in the Spiritan International School of Theology (SIST), Attakwu, Nigeria.

**Rev. Father Humphrey Uchenna Ani**, Ph.D. is the Head, Department of Philosophy (and teaches Philosophy in the same Department) Bigard Memorial Seminary, Enugu.

**Rev. Father Modestus Anyaegbu** Ph.D. teaches Philosophy in the Pope John Paul II Seminary, Awka.

**Rev. Father Chrysanthus Nnaemeka Ogbozo,** Ph.D. teaches Philosophy in the Department of Philosophy, University of Nigeria Nsukka, Nigeria.

**Rev. Father Sylvanus Ifeanyichukwu Nnoruka,** Professor, teaches Philosophy in the Department of Philosophy, Faculty of Arts, Chukwuemeka Odumegwu Ojukwu University, Igbariam Campus, Nigeria.

# Chapter 1

# African Communalism and the Quest for Sustainable Development in Africa

Fabian Ikechukwu Agudosy

## Abstract

It is still a worrisome issue that despite so many conferences, seminars, workshops, etc. held in a bid to bring about sustainable development in Africa, such efforts have not yielded the expected results. That is why this paper is an attempt to view and review how sustainable development can be attained for the benefit of the African peoples. Many scholars have equally proffered varied solutions that will make sustainable development *a fait accompli*, but some of these solutions have been vitiated in their methods and/or operations because they are not rooted in our culture. In this write-up, the author advocates that proper adherence to, and adoption of African communalism will be profitable in bringing about sustainable development in Africa.

**Key words:** African communalism, sustainable development, quest, Nigeria

## Introduction

So far, many countries in Africa (Nigeria inclusive) have had the opportunity of discussing how they could bring about sustainable development in their countries. Many avenues have been explored, all to raise the standard of living of the populace. But quite unfortunately, most of these attempts (if not all) have met their waterloo, yielding no profitable harvest to the planners as well as the populace who are basically the recipients of such sustainable development. Some of these countries have even invited seasoned experts and promising foreign investors from Europe, America, Asia and so on, to come and salvage their economy in order to draw their countries from palpable economic doldrums. Some in the name of "foreign investment" have boldly called for the need and even utilized the profitable wealth of knowledge of the foreign investors in order to improve their economic prowess, yet we hear the same ugly story about not attaining sustainable economic development.

Besides, our political office holders have not helped any the better to streamline numerous development projects along our indigenous cultures. In their insouciance, they merely adopt questionable foreign policies that momentarily pay them off and satisfy their egocentric needs. To worsen the matter, they apply the politics of brute force without relying on the autochthonous cultures and values simply to appear relevant to their western counterparts. As Mogomme Masoga and Hassan Kaya rightly observed, "The prevailing paradigm of development in Africa suffers from relying too much on coercion and authoritarianism, which arises from African leaders who are using force to maintain power in the face of vanishing legitimacy."[1]

It becomes necessary to examine how we can achieve sustainable development in Africa via African communalism which, it is believed, will be a veritable solution to our age-long quest to attain sustainable development. This idea is based on the belief that in Africa, communalism had been a profitable way of improving the livelihood of all and sundry, no matter one's social standing. The leader usually considered the led as human beings who should be given every support in order to live decent life. He viewed the primary purpose of his assuming any political office as a way of improving the livelihood of his subjects and not to lord it over them and intimidate them. As such, so long as one remains in the community and abides by the norms of the community, one's interests are thereby protected.

As a matter of fact, it is our abandonment of communalism for individualism that pitifully paved way for numerable problems and hardships as they are witnessed today in Africa. Thus, people are no longer concerned with the welfare of their fellow men and women. Their interest is focused on themselves and for themselves, and how to feather their own nest even to the detriment of their fellow men and women. It does not require any extraordinary proof to convince us that such way of life is a deviation from the traditional standard, where mutual cooperation is the watchword. Surely, it is greed that makes us feel that we can achieve any feat without others and that we can live without others. What a utopian expectation! According to Nze, "A solitary individual is an absurdity. A solitary individual dances carrying his bag – an infamous thing to do – a cursed life indeed. It is even a sad thing for the spirits that kill off their own people."[2]

The basic cause of this aberration – the neglect of communalism – is the abandonment of our belief systems, cultures, values as well as the norms of our land. These norms give strong support to the practice of communalism as against individualism, which has not only stampeded the possibility of any sustainable development in Africa but is also considered a thoughtless aberration. As Nze remarks, "The present individualistic lifestyle of the African is a deviant life. It is a perverted life brought about by the relegation to the background of the African belief and religion that acted as a protection and sanction."[3] No doubt, it is this seemingly irreversible shift from communalism to individualism that has crippled almost every conceivable success in attaining sustainable development in Africa. It is because of this that no formidable effort made to bring about sustainable development has yielded the expected positive results. This is because the deviation is characterized by neglect of the poor, the environment, agriculture, health services, hunting, fishing, forestry, the population growth, unemployment, etc. It is hopeful that a reversal to the old system – communalism – will help to cement every conceivable and strategic plan toward achieving sustainable development,

**Reviewing Communalism and Sustainable Development**
Communalism is a way of life which was originally and commonly found among Africans, hence the name "African communalism." It is a way of life in which the individual subsumes his personal interests to those of the community. It is a unique force that binds the individuals in the community in the form of brotherhood with the ultimate end of securing the well-being of all persons in the community. In this case, communalism is community oriented. As Agudosy remarks, "It depicts mutual participation and equal sharing of certain fundamental cultural

and autochthonous values or goods in the community."[4] Some of these basic cultural values include "wholesome human relations" among people, community fellow-feeling, as mostly reflected in communal land tenure and ownership", "live-and-let-live" philosophy, altruism (including medical and economic variants of it) and "hospitality."[5] It may be likened to the early biblical apostolic Church where the brethren "who believed were of one heart and soul, and no one said that any of the things which he possessed was his own, but they had everything in common."[6] Those who had excess of the world's goods gave out their abundance for the benefit of the have-nots who had virtually nothing. In fact, it was "from each according to his ability, to each according to his needs."

This communalistic way of life was depicted in Achebe's *magnum opus, Things Fall Apart*, where "a clan which once thought like one, spoke like one, shared a common awareness and acted like one"[7] lost its unity with the coming of the white men. No doubt, it was the influx of the white men with their western education that brought about the almost disintegration of communalism and overwhelmingly replaced it with individualism. Not only that they brought western education, which invariably made it possible for their development programmes to be Eurocentric and willy-nilly downplaying Afrocentric quest for development. To make it possible for them to debase African cultures and values, especially the ones intricately tied to African communalistic life, they initiated the concept of globalization, which has left an average African nation in economic strangulation. This is because with globalization, "the freedom of developing countries to make policies for the economic and political growth of their counties are [sic] lost."[8] This approach to life has affected the concept of development where the preoccupation is on making it at one's personal effort. With this, we may ask: What is development?

Development is a concept that has received numerous interpretations, some of which are limited in scope. Traditionally, Todaro and Smith defined development as "achieving sustained rates of growth of income per capita to enable a nation to expand its output at a rate faster than the growth rate of its population."[9] It is in this sense that development is conceived in terms of economic growth. Thus, whenever the concept of development is discussed, it is frequently interpreted from the economic point of view. That is why some scholars suggest that it is preferable to talk about economic development instead of development *simpliciter*. Their underlying supposition is that whatever form of development that is conceived, it has its fulcrum as economic development. Thus, economic development is simply defined as "the sustained, concerted efforts of policymakers and community to promote the standard of living and economic health in a specific area."[10] Here, there are two stress areas – standard of living and economic health. As such, whenever there is a massive improvement in these areas, we can say there is economic development. Such economic development must clearly reflect in the way of life of the citizens in terms of improved quality of life of the citizenry. It is, no doubt, in the context of economic development that Nwankwo opines that "development is basically about attaining a level of socio-economic performance that leads to improved quality of life of the citizenry: improvement in the national welfare."[11] Goldstein refers to it as "the combined processes of capital accumulation, rising per capita incomes (with consequent falling birth rates), increasing skills in the population, adoption of new technological styles, and other related social and economic changes."[12]

However, this conception of development is considered lopsided and inadequate in elucidating the nitty-gritty involved in such omnibus concept. Owing to the inherent lapses in this traditional conception of development, a new economic and more acceptable view of development came up, which considers development as "the reduction or elimination of poverty, inequality, and unemployment within the context of a growing economy".[13]

Aside from this conception, another more acceptable view of development was given by Gyekye, who eloquently contends that "to be developed is to have the capability to perform the functions appropriate to the object, such as society or institution, said to be developed."[14] According to Gyekye:

> The capability of an object to perform its functions manifests itself in several ways, which include: demonstrating signs of high degrees of independence, self-sufficiency and self-reliance, being able to face serious challenges to its existence – social, political,

economic, etc.; fending for itself; being able to feed itself and control its environment, demonstrating signs of inventiveness and innovativeness, an [sic] so forth.[15]

It is in this context that we can appreciate Walter Rodney's contention that "Development means a capacity for self-sustaining growth."[16] What it entails is that an economy must have to register advances which in turn will go to promote further progress. As we know too well that most African countries still struggle to reduce poverty level, inequality, and unemployment, it boils down that they are far from attaining development much less sustainable development. The combined effect of these definitions *supra* is that these African countries have not been capable to perform the functions appropriate to them by their inability to eliminate poverty and provide jobs for their citizenry. It becomes necessary to succinctly posit Dudley Seers' basic question about the meaning of development:

> The questions to ask about a country's development are therefore: What has been happening to poverty? What has been happening to unemployment? What has been happening to inequality? If all three of these have declined from high levels, then beyond doubt this has been a period of development for the country concerned. If one or two of these central problems have been growing worse, especially if all three have, it would be strange to call the result "development" even if per capita income doubled.[17]

It suffices to note, at this juncture, that this latter conception of development has been faithfully adopted, for brevity's sake, in the entire paper.

Sustainable development (or preferably, sustainable economic development (SED)) is a term used synonymously with the term "sustainability" and has often been used that way. It is often broken down into three constituent parts, viz., environmental sustainability, economic sustainability, and socio-political sustainability. Added to this typology is the cultural sustainability, which makes all of them to be classified as the four pillars of sustainable development. This last arm was made possible with the Universal Declaration on Cultural Diversity.

Sustainability generally refers to "meeting the needs of the present generation without compromising the needs of the future generations."[18] Thus, a development path is said to be sustainable "if and only if the stock of overall capital assets remains constant or rises over time."[19] Sustainable development is "a pattern of resources use that aims to meet human needs while preserving the environment."[20] For there to be SED, the basic human needs of the populace must be adequately met.[21] Unfortunately, Nigeria was classified by World Bank as one of the lower-middle-income countries (LMCs).[22]

So, in order to ensure that there would be SED, with the assurance of basic human needs, the focus should be on children, for they are "central to meeting a population's basic needs."[23] To achieve this objective, education, coupled with the ancillary aid of the Internet, stands as the best bet. With education, the hope of meeting up with other basic needs and moving through the demographic transition is assured.[24]

Broadly speaking, "the sustainable development mantra enjoins current generations to take a systems approach to growth and development and to manage natural, produced, and social capital for the welfare of their own and future generations."[25] In the words of Needham, it is "the ability to meet the needs of the present while contributing to the future generations' needs."[26]

One of the most widely recognised definitions of sustainable development was given by Gro Harlem Brundtland who defines it as "development that meets the needs of the present without compromising the ability of future generations to meet their own needs."[27] However, most definitions of sustainable development usually consider the need for future generation. Winberly as cited in Omotayo suggested that "to be sustainable is to provide for food, fibre, and other natural and social resources needed for survival for a group and to provide it in such a manner that maintains the essential resources for present and future generations."[28] This entails that it is not enough to have rapid economic development, but such development also has to make provision for the future generation. Some of the attributes of development that make them sustainable are articulated by Ogu and Adeniji as cited by Kadiri as follows:

(i)   The development activity does not damage natural resources (and social systems);

(ii)  Physical development activity ensures net positive impact on natural resources and

(iii) Should not damage the natural resources necessary to sustain it.[29]

**Communalism in the Context of Sustainable Development**

The current trend toward the attainment of sustainable development in Africa has invariably led us to imbibe and assimilate foreign policies and ideologies of the West with their attendant shortcomings. This has made us to almost forget our rich cultural heritage and its underpinnings and forcefully trying to imbibe a strange and new mode of life that leaves the purportedly poor African masses impoverished. Our political office holders have equally worsened the matter by their complicity and/or conspiracy of silence simply because their loaves of bread are buttered in that regard. Without paying a careful regard to communalistic life of the Africans as well as their cultural values, sustainable development will simply be a zoomy mirage. As Mogomme Masoga and Hassan Kaya rightly observed:

> We cannot significantly advance the development of Africa unless those involved in the development process of the continent take African societies and cultures seriously, as they are, not as they ought to be or even as they might be; and that sustainable development is never going to occur unless we build on the indigenous, i.e., what the local communities know and can afford.[30]

Unlike the Westerners, Africans live communitarian lifestyle. This is clearly depicted in the spirit of "live and let live." This cooperative spirit, what in management sciences is called "team spirit", enables each person to have a fair share of the proceeds generated as a result of such cooperative spirit in almost every facet of their life. That is why in the real African milieu, labour was cheap and meritocracy was encouraged and cherished. People were not allowed to reap where they did not sow. Such challenging attitude to life encourages diligence in labour as labour is no longer viewed as punishment or, less happily, suffering. Chinua Achebe insightfully painted a very good picture of what the Africans abhorred in the person of Unoka, who was referred to as poor, a failure and a loafer[31], and eventually died without a title and was also heavily in debt. Achebe, however, contrasted the character of Unoka with that of Okonkwo his son, whose fame, as he put it, "rested on solid personal achievements" and it "had grown like a bush-fire in the harmattan."[32]

One important aspect of African communalism that is highly regarded is the establishment of the family. Any people that abhor the family are bound to atrophy. The family is the basic social unit of the society. Family tie in African society is extraordinarily strong. Marriage is not an affair of a young man and his fiancée as it is obtainable in Western society. It is a long process between both families of the man and woman. Life is not an individual venture. According to Arinze, "For the Igbos, as for many Africans, to exist is to live in the group, to see things with the group, to do things with the group."[33] This team spirit immeasurably brings about development and progress in the society. It is not yet known in the history of humanity where individualism thrived better than communalism. That is why there is an organization, made up of different people with clearly specified functions so that particular intended goals would be met. This explains why the family, as a basic social organization, is cherished and encouraged in the African society.

Communitarian lifestyle of traditional African society also enhances community development. For instance, Africans in traditional African society help one another to build houses and other community projects like constructing roads, funeral ceremonies, marriage, farming and so on. As Ottenberg remarks:

> Villagers compete to build the first and best schools, village groups, to improve the market. Many social groups strive to push some of their talented sons ahead in schooling and to obtain scholarship in competition with other groups. Individuals who acquire scholarship, wealth or political influence are expected to use their social stand for the benefit of the group with which they are associated.[34]

This social union brought about the existence of innumerable societies like age group (*otu ogbo*), kindred family union (*umunna*), women genealogical lineage (*umu-okpu*), titled men (*nze-na-ozo* society). Such societies promote social co-existence of individuals and well-being of the society. They ensure the smooth running of affairs of the community by collecting taxes, help in recovering levies as and when imposed by the government and towns, reprimands and forestalls behaviour that are inimical to the well-being of kindreds.[35] Hence, they promote ideas that will enhance the good and amicable co-existence of different units.

Age group is an old social institution which constitutes an indispensable tool of good government and hence forming a vital component of administrative machinery for sustaining the well-being of many Igbo societies.[36] In like manner, the *umu-okpu* help to settle issues in matters affecting deaths and second burial rites, and also in wedding and settling frictions existing among their men folks. Moreover, titled men group (the *Nze-na-Ozo* society) form the framework that handles problems threatening the internal and external political, social and economic well-being of the community prior to the advent of colonial government of Africa, these include settling land disputes and other cases considered inimical to the maintenance of peace and order in the town. Unfortunately, in the current situation of Africa, settling of dispute especially the one pertaining to land has been distorted as people lose their lives in the course of land dispute while others are rendered useless by their rivals. The reason is simply because sincerity and truthfulness are no longer cherished values as people prefer to tell lies to obtain excessive, though inordinate, material gains.

One important factor, which is the backbone of sustainable development, rests on the sense of life and its value. Africans value and cherish life more than any other thing. This value system cuts across every African country and tribe. To express and concretize this value system, they name their children *Nduka* (life is greater than wealth), *Nduka ego* (life *is* greater than money) or *Nwakaego* (human life is greater than money), and so many other appellations depending on how life is viewed and cherished. The implication of this value system is that nothing can make an African take the life of his brethren no matter what condition he finds himself. As such, any development plan that does not take the life of humans as its priority cannot be upheld in Africa. That is the sense in which it is said that development is human-centred.

Unfortunately, this has been the major problem Africa has to contend with as there is already a paradigm shift from the sense of "being" to the sense of "having", making people to cherish property rather than cherishing and protecting the life of the people. That is why, at present, there is not yet sustainable development in Africa. The reason is quite obvious as we have downplayed the essence of life and are claiming to mindlessly acquire wealth.

**Education and Sustainable Development in Africa**

How do we ensure that sustainable development becomes a reality in Africa? One major way of doing it is through constant education of the peoples on the need to cherish life first. Indeed, "using education to achieve sustainable development is possible through creating public awareness, knowledge, and conviction on how to achieve a sustainable condition."[37] However, the task is daunting if the educators do not take into consideration the life patterns and autochthonous values of the recipients. The African sense of life is quite informative as a guide to living. The African sees himself as living his life in the community with other members of the community. It is such life that is the determinant factor of any project that is to be carried out. That is why excessive materialism or mere physical development does not make for sustainable development; rather, it debases human life. That is why communalism, with all its vagaries, should be encouraged in Africa.

The seed of discord planted by the West in Africa in their quest for globalization (unification) will never bring sustainable development. As Masoga and Kaya righty remarked:

> Globalization, through its sheer power, reinforces images of global uniformity, imposes its own version of knowledge about Africa to all parts of the world, but at the same time increasingly denies Africa a global space to produce the truthful knowledge of itself.[38]

Whichever way we view our contact with the West, it is obvious that we need not accept whatever developmental project they bring to us. For instance, in the case of globalization, we ought to find out why they are conscientiously championing it and what we stand to gain or lose as a continent before participating actively in it. Even the concept of glocalization, which the sociologist Roland Robertson coined in the Harvard Business Review in 1980, to describe the development and distribution of global concepts, products, and services to fit into local contexts they are sold and used in, is and may not be a convenient escape route as it also has the tendency of denying Africa, as a continent, her main sources of wealth.

Again, it is very obvious that educational system in Africa today is purely western-oriented, and the language of its operation is equally done with western languages. We should not lose sight of the fact that language underlies the culture of a people. It basically depicts what they are and what they are known for in the midst of the peoples of the world. According to M'Bayo, Nwokeafor and Onwumechili, "Language, particularly, has been critical in mass mobilization and education, which are imperatives for development."[39]

Unfortunately, Africans have given themselves the impression, mostly in their conduct, that they are of inferior race and that is why there is gradual abandonment of our language, our religion, our polity, our wealth (i.e., natural resources) and of course, our lives for the West. What a shameful type of life! That is why an African who has no source of living, for instance, prefers to die in Europe, Asia, America, etc. instead of coming back to Africa and leaning on his brethren for assistance.

It is no longer news that a good number of people from Africa have turned other continents into graveyards as they prefer to die there instead of coming back home. Where lies the urge to sustain the development of Africa when there is profound exodus of children of Africa to other continents in search of greener pastures instead of returning home for us to strategize ways of boosting our economy with our acquired knowledge made possible through education? Without adhering to the right principles underlying our culture, especially our communalistic life, there may not be sustainable development in Africa even as her debt as a whole is frequently increasing geometrically with the passage of time as a result of bad leaders who prefer to feather their nest and those of their friends and cohorts, leaving the majority of Africans to live from hand to mouth.

As a matter of fact, we must reiterate the importance of education in addressing and redressing the current trend whereby sustainable development is viewed in terms of structural or physical development, which may not have any reasonable impact on the lives of the populace. That is why education, both formal and informal, must be stepped up to break the jinx making it extremely difficult to attain the required development. It becomes, therefore, imperative to educate the peoples on their culture and cultural values. So many means may be adopted in this regard, even the use of the mass media, especially radio and television.

There is also the need to adopt mainly the dominant local languages in transmission and give minimal percent of the time to foreign languages. Surely, mass media are known to "play a key role in promoting a greater degree of participation of the population in facilitating the democratic process within the framework of sustainable development."[40] Thus, as engines of change as well as actively involved in educating people in literacy programmes, the mass media are expected "to extend public education and promote innovation in agriculture, health practice, population control, and other social economic matters."[41]

Although in using the local languages as tools for sustainable development, there may be foreseeable handicaps as to whose language and cultural values would be promoted in multi-cultural and multi-lingual nations in Africa, it equally calls for proper scheduling in radio and television to give each cultural group the presence required.


## Conclusion

Any quest for sustainable development in Africa must have to consider the autochthonous cultures of the Africans. Sustainable development cannot be *a fait accompli* if all the West will give us is a borrowed and imposed development paradigm, which will not take root in Africa. Their plan in bringing us development programmes is merely to keep Africa perpetually enslaved. A particularly good example of enslavement meant to perpetually keep Africa backward in development is the use of satellite TV. As Khor rightly remarks, "The establishment of satellite TV and the availability of small receivers, and the spread of the use of electronic mail and Internet make it difficult for governments to determine cultural or communication policy, or to control the spread of information and cultural products."[42] Such a shift of emphasis from local programmes to foreign programmes, which are readily available and uncontrollable, has made it difficult for us to inculcate the African values in our people, and this is one of the evils of globalization. That is why there is need for a change of method of imparting the knowledge of African cultural values to our people through the community radios so as to bring about sustainable development in the near future.

Until there is increasing recognition of the indigenous patterns of life in the political, socio-economic, and religious aspects of our lives as Africans, there may not be any hope of sustainable development in Africa. That is why, for any development in Africa to yield some benefits, such development needs to be localized, i.e., to be attuned to Africans' ways of life and relying on local resources. This is one particular area many successive leaders in Africa have failed. Hence, a clarion call for sustainable development is welcome through the indigenization of our current system of governance.

# References


1. Masoga, A. M., & Kaya, H., "Building on the Indigenous: An Appropriate Paradigm for Sustainable Development in Africa." In G. Walmsley (Ed.), *African Philosophy and the Future of Africa*, U.S.A.: The Council for Research in Values and Philosophy, 2011, p. 153.

2. Nze, C. B., *Aspects of African Communalism.* Onitsha: Veritas Press, p. 7.

3. *Ibid.*, p. 9.

4. Agudosy, F. I., "Nze on Communalism and Communication." In I. Odimegwu (Ed.), *Perspectives on African Communalism.* Canada: Trafford Publishing, 2007, p. 484.

5. Sofola, J. A., *African Culture and the African Personality.* Ibadan, 1982, p. 52.

6. Bible, The Reversed Standard Version. Acts 4:32.

7. Achebe, C., *Things Fall Apart.* London: Heinemann Educational Books, 1980, p. v.

8. Odia, S. I., "Globalization and African Philosophy." J. A. Agbakoba (Eds.), *Philosophy and Praxis in Africa*, Ibadan: Hope Publications, 2006, p. 278.

9. Todaro, M. P., & Smith, S. C., *Economic Development, 11$^{th}$ ed.*, England: Pearson Education, 2011, p. 14.

10. Wikipedia, "Sustainable Development." Retrieved on July 31, 2018 from http://en.wikipedia.org/wiki/sustainable_development.

11. Nwankwo, O. B. C., "Good Governance Matters for Development." In O. S.A. Obikeze, A. Akamobi, C. J. Nwanegbo, & C. Nwabueze (Eds.), *Dynamics of Public Sector Management in Nigeria.* Enugu: Rhyce Kerex, 2009, p. 17.

12. Goldstein, J. S., *International Relations, 5$^{th}$ ed.*, Delhi, India: Pearson Education, 2003, p. 495.

13. Todaro, M. P., & Smith, S. C., *Op. Cit.*, p. 15.

14. Gyekye, K., *The Unexamined Life: Philosophy and the African Experience.* Accra, Ghana: Sankofa Publishing Co., 1996, p. 17.

15. *Ibid.*, pp. 17 – 18.

16. Rodney, W., "Technological Stagnation and Economic Distortion in Pre-colonial Times." In P. C. W. Gutkind, & P. Waterman (Ed.), African *Social Studies: A Radical Reader.* London: Heinemann, 1981, p. 108.

17. Seers, D., "The Meaning of Development." Paper presented at the Eleventh World Conference of the Society for International Development, New Delhi, 1969, p. 3. As cited in Todaro, M. P. & Smith, S. C., *Op. Cit.*, p. 15.

18. World Commission on Environment and Development. *Our Common Future.* New York: Oxford University Press, 1987, p. 4. As cited in Todaro, M. P., & Smith, S. C. *Op. Cit.*, p. 467.

19. Pearce, D. W., & Warford, J. J., *World without End: Economics, Environment, and Sustainable Development – A Summary.* Washington, D. C.: World Bank, 1990, p. 2.

20. Wikipedia, Sustainable development. Retrieved on July 31, 2018. *Op. Cit.*

21. Streeten, et al., *First Things First: Meeting Basic Human Needs in the Developed Countries*, New York: Oxford University Press. As cited in Goldstein, J. S., *Op. Cit.*, p. 474.

22. World Bank, *World Development Indicators*, Washington D.C.: World Bank.

23. Goldstein, J. S., *Op. Cit.*, p. 474.

24. Noor, A., *Education and Basic Human Needs*, Washington, D.C.: World Bank. As cited in Goldstein, J. S., *Op. Cit.*, p. 474.

25. Wikipedia, "Sustainable Development." Retrieved on July 31, 2018. *Op. Cit.*

26. Needham, M. T., "A Psychological Approach to a Thriving Resilient Community." *International Journal of Business Humanities and Technology, 1* (3). Retrieved on July 31, 2018 from html://en.wikipedia.org/wiki/sustainable_development

27. Wikipedia, "Sustainable Development," *Op. Cit.*, p. 2.

28. Winberly, R. C., "Policy Perspectives on Social, Agricultural and Rural Sustainability. Presidential Address to the 55th Annual Meeting of the Rural Sociological Society, August 16, 1992," pp. 1-29. As cited in Omotayo, A., "Perspectives on Rural Development in Nigeria." In L. Oso (Ed.) *Communication and Development: A Reader*, Abeokuta: Jedidiah Publishers, 2002, p. 35.

29. Kadira, W. A., "The Environment and Development: Securing the Future." In L. Oso (Ed.) *Communication and Development: A Reader, Op. Cit.*, pp. 49 – 50.

30. Masoga, A. M., & Kaya, H., *Ibid.*

31. Achebe, C., *Op. Cit.*, p. 4.

32. *Ibid.*, p. 3

33. Arinze, F. A., *Sacrifice in Igbo Religion*. Ibadan: University Press, 1970, pp. 3 – 4.

34. Ottenberg, S., "Igbo Receptivity to Change." In *Continuity and Change*, London: Oxford University Press, 1967, p. 137.

35. Ogbukagu, I. N., *Traditional Igbo Belief and Practices*. Owerri: Novelty Industrial Enterprise, 1997, pp. 55 – 56.

36. Basden, G. T., *Niger Ibos*. London: Frankcass & Co., 1966, p. 194.

37. M'Bayo, R., Nwokeafor, C., & Onwumechili, C., "Press Freedom and the Imperatives of Democracy: Towards Sustainable Development." In *African Media Review*, Vol. 9, No. 3, 199, p. 37.

38. Masoga, A. M., & Kaya, H., *Op. Cit.*, p. 158.

39. M'Bayo, R., Nwokeafor, C., & Onwumechili, C., *Ibid.*

40. *Ibid.*, p. 49.

41. McQuail, D., *McQuail's Mass Communication Theory, 2nd edition*, London: Sage Publications, 1987, p. 97.

42. Khor, M., *Globalisation and the South: Some Critical Issues*, Ibadan: Spectrum Books, p. 4.

# Chapter 2

# Democracy and Freedom:
# Towards a Redefinition of Nigerian Democracy

Kevin Udewagu

## Introduction

On the 27 of December 2018, a friend's car broke down in our village market square. As he sought for solutions to fix his car, a group of men in a Toyota Hilux (with marked plate number) arrived on the scene. They demanded that he must move his car for them to drive through (as owners of the land). My friend requested of them to swerve right or left and get going for there was enough space for them to do so. But they insisted on his moving the car to the surprise of all around that scene. Why would the gentleman in question stand there if that car could be moved simply as they demanded? However, the altercation between them gathered a huge crowd when the driver of the Hilux van, though in nonmilitary outfit, threatened my friend, letting him understand that he is in Nigeria, where freedom is limited to and interpreted by "those who belong". The above incident spurred me to write this article in order to present the absolute need to redefine our concept of democracy in the light of the democratic principle of freedom. The narrative above is but a tip of the iceberg of how some, if not most of those who make and enforce our laws, understand democratic rule and its principle of freedom. In their perception of democracy, common good is sacrificed at the altar of individual ego.

Be that as it may, democracy in Nigeria has recorded remarkable progress since independence. Among other things, military juntas hopefully now belong to history, and our people, at least in principle, have a say in the affairs of their political community, because according to Salkever, politics is a participatory way of life.[4] Not minding the recorded progress made, lots of questions remain unanswered regarding our understanding and application of democracy. The questions have arisen from the apparent irregularities displayed in the just concluded 2019 general elections. Remarkably there was the sense of insecurity that impeded people's freedom of choice (a fundamental principle of democracy) in all its ramifications. How can we talk of democracy when citizens are afraid of performing their civic duties (voting and being voted for)? Do we talk of democracy when they are afraid of criticizing a regime? Do we talk of freedom when a citizen is afraid to go to his/her farmland or visit a friend within his community? It is more difficult to talk of democracy when citizens are convinced that their votes do not count and that they therefore have no say in matters concerning the affairs of their state. What then is democracy? What is the place of freedom in democracy?

## Concept of Democracy and Freedom

An average reader when confronted with the question of what democracy is will contently align himself with the famous political dictum of Abraham Lincoln, who defined democracy as government of the people, by the people and for the people. Lincoln's words captured the concept of democracy as people oriented. It also alludes to freedom as an essential principle of democracy; depicting the people's capacity to determine the way they conduct their affairs (within a political community) for the common good of life. In other words, democracy is an organized system of living/rule that originates from the people and falls back to them as well. This is further elucidated by an explanation of the component root terms of democracy. Scholars argue that democracy is derived from the Greek terms; *demos* and *kratos*. *Demos* is used either to designate a village as the smallest administrative unit in the Greek world (Athens) or it is used to designate the people of Athens collectively. *Kratos*, on its part, means power/authority. In a nutshell, democracy relates that power/authority belongs to the people.

In order to give relevance to this literary piece, we limit ourselves to the second usage of *demos* in relation to the collective people, i.e., an

---

[4]Stephen G. Salkever, "Women, Soldiers, and Citizens: Plato and Aristotle on Political Virility," Polity 19, no. 2 (winter 1986) p. 232.

opportunity for male (Athenian) adult citizens to speak their minds regarding the affairs of their community. But applied to Nigeria's political context and community, *demos* is an opportunity for adult Nigerian citizens irrespective of gender, tribe and religious affiliations to actively participate in all facets of our political life and affairs, because it is a civic role enjoyed by every citizen of any democratic regime. This important civic role of every citizen recalls Aristotle's reason for reforming democracy in his treatise the *Politics* – good life. Aristotle's reform was concerned with the place of the *demos*? And what they should do within their democratic setup? Without adequately answering these fundamental questions, every democratic regime lacks legitimacy and it cannot be for the well-being of its people. Hence, the well-being of the people stands as the measure of a good regime. Curiously, is that the case of the ordinary people within the ambience of Nigerian democracy? What common good is available to the average Nigerian? These questions are pertinent because in Nigerian democracy, power seems not to reside with the people for them to exercise freely their rights and freedom in order to enjoy the ends of politics – good life. Politics for the good life of the people is so important that Maritain defines democracy as "a regime wherein the people enjoy their social and political majority and exercise it to conduct their own affairs."[5] Consequently, where the average citizens of a nation have the ability to exercise their own affairs, democracy and freedom conflate for their own good.

The term freedom can be viewed from the translation of the Greek term *eleutheria*.[6] It means that the citizens have certain inalienable rights like right to life, holding public office, freedom of speech, movement, etc. These rights and privileges of citizens gained through freedom informs the reason why Aristotle in the *Politics* interprets freedom as the basic principle and driving force of democracy.[7] Given that democracy is

---

[5] Jacques Maritain, *Christianity and Democracy. The Rights of Man and The Natural Law*, tr. Doris C. Anson, San Francisco, Ignatius Press, p. 44.

[6] "Eleutheria is defined as freedom; being in control of one's life; having sole authority in all respects; power to do what one likes in life; being unsparing in using and possessing property." Cfr. Plato, Definitions, *in Complete Works of Plato eds*. John M. Cooper, D. S. Hutchinson, Indianapolis, Hackett, 1997, 412d.

predicated on the principle of freedom, a regime cannot claim to be democratic without ensuring and defending the freedom of its citizens. With freedom as a foundation on which other characteristics of democracy are based, it serves as the aim/end of democracy. The end is realized when the citizens of a nation freely express their choice of who or what they want to shape their socio-political life, either through the aspect of political rule or living according to one's fancy. Political rule as an aspect of democratic freedom implies ruling and being ruled in turn. It validates one's citizenship giving it the capacity to partake in administration of justice and to qualify for election into political offices. This distinguishes citizens from resident aliens who though have defined legal rights are constrained in certain areas. Another aspect of democratic freedom is living according to one's fancy. It portrays the citizen as a free born and not a slave. Viewed from its Greek origin, slaves are not free to live as they want because they are another's property. But living as one pleases in Nigeria seems to underline our wrong understanding and application of democratic concept of freedom especially by those constituted into government. Those in elective democratic leadership easily forget the plight of the ordinary citizen no sooner than they occupy their political offices. This political attitude reflects in the action of the young man in our introductory narrative, who demonstrates how government official convoy motorcades abuse ordinary road users. Nevertheless, it also goes beyond that. The oppression of the ordinary citizens by elected Nigerians includes the paltry sum negotiated as minimum wage for the workers, while the so called elected who purportedly come into office to serve the people loot the national treasury dry for their personal pockets through various clandestine means. It is for instance disgusting to hear of the outrageous salary paid to the members of the Nigerian National House of Assembly. All these allude to the abuse of democratic principles by political office holders. Their primary object in government is their personal comfort instead of the end of politics – happiness for all. Such denigrative conception of political leadership calls for a revaluation of our present structure of political governance.

## A Critical Survey of Nigerian Experience/Experiment

---

[7] "The basic premise of a democratic sort of regime is freedom." Cfr. Aristotle, Politics, VI, 2. 1317a 40.

Democracy in Nigeria is, to say the least, at crossroads. Anoje-Eke reasons beyond my perspective. For him, it is the nation that is at crossroads, consequent on the type of politics played along ethnic and religious sentiments which work against response to national questions and problems.[8] I concur with Anoje-Eke, when the principle of the relationship between the parts and the whole is applied. When the whole is in decay, the constitutive parts will almost definitely not be in-tact. However, in our search for a remedy, we trace the cause of the malaise.

After fifty-nine years of independence, the political class is yet to display a blueprint of their understanding, interpretation and adaptation of democratic rule. This is because they either do not understand democratic rule or they lack the political will to effectively apply standard democratic principles in their leadership positions. Principles that will initiate, implement and perpetuate constructive changes in Nigeria for national and futuristic growth. Those who constitute the political class in Nigeria cannot be considered thorough statesmen but businessmen. For instance, a statesman (politician) would stand by his party manifesto and work toward carrying such to national levels for the common and national good. The contrary prevails in Nigeria. Elected officials dump their parties to join the winning party. Their reasons are anything but the national interest and progress. This accounts for instability and the apparent stagnation of our democratic growth and maturity.

Reasons for this anomaly are not far-fetched. Among other things, the incursion of the military into politics played a major role in this nationally embarrassing political orientation. Between political independence and the last military regime in 1998, political power resided more among the military than the political class. This has had negative consequences on the psyche of the nation. Iloegbunam captures the negative implications of military involvement in the Nigerian political life when he said: "Nigeria sank in world esteem because, in the face of the global march to democracy, its people have continued to groan under military dictatorship peculiar for its mindless brutality."[9] The late General S. Abacha regime epitomized the blazing

---

[8] Joe Anoje-Eke, *A Nation at Cross-roads. The Way Forward*, Enugu, Catholic Diocesan Printing Press, 2018, p. 3.

[9] Chuks Iloegbunam, Tell Magazine, No 4, January 22, 1996, p. 5.

nature of military regimes and their brutality. In fact, General Ibrahim Babangida's and Abacha's military rule reduced the national psyche of a Nigerian to the *tokunbo* mentality that shapes an average Nigerian's mindset. The military rulers flagrantly abused power, neglected rule of law, and consequently infringed on fundamental rights of Nigerians. Unfortunately, military intervention in Nigerian politics happened at the nascent stage of our democratic drives. Hence, the military laid an anti-progress social and political foundation that the country still grapples with. They did not only enthrone and sustain corruption but also destroyed true federalism which under the regional system had spurred massive competitive drives and development across the nation. Disgracefully, the current body of politicians have seemingly sustained and perpetuated the socio and political systems and structures that the military governments instituted. The so-called democratic leaders have done very little to correct the anomalies of the military in governance.

With the military outside the corridors of governance, hopes were high. But the hopes have been quickly dashed because of the ugly realities confronting the people: realities arising from retrogression rather than progression. The only seeming gains from the governance of politicians are Nigerians' claim to practice democracy, at least in principle. They now have elected governments, like in the general elections of 2019 where it seems opportunities were availed the people to perform their civic rights of electing officials into offices. However, democracy is not all about electioneering. It is more about the end of politics – good life for the people. A good life that engenders from the activities that are determined by the freedom of the people (if their common will is respected) to choose their elected representatives. This freedom of choice has failed in Nigeria and the electioneering process in Nigeria has become more of 'selectioneering'. Hence, the wrong people are selected through rigging and undemocratic processes into governance. Having acquired powers through crooked means, such politicians see and interpret themselves as demi-gods who must be worshipped by the people. This leads them to abuse their power. Such political disposition is a threat to our democracy. The long-term impact of bad political leadership is the existence of impoverished people at the mercy of their leaders for their daily bread. The harsh social and economic conditions caused by bad governance have been openly expressed in the dissatisfaction of Nigerians, a dissatisfaction that is about to threaten the unity and integrity of the nation. And this has led to the growing wave of agitation for secession which can be encouraged in the face of the disgraceful shambles called 2019 elections.

Jacques Maritain's definition of democracy as "a regime wherein the people enjoy their social and political majority and exercise it to conduct their own affairs" serves as a point of departure for our critical analysis of Nigerian democracy. This definition also characterizes the weakness of our democracy, because the people are not actively involved in Nigerian democracy. The people hardly enjoy their social and political majority. They do not even have the freedom to express their issues and voice their concerns as the majority. Painfully, Nigerians are denied their mutual need based on necessity – need for exchange of skills and services for supply of daily needs. For instance, in the present democratic regime, human life and its social nature have been so devalued by incessant killing of innocent citizens by terrorist groups – Boko haram – whose activities, so unchecked, have paralyzed the country as evident in reduction in inter-state movement and high cost of food stuff due to low productivity. The Fulani herdsmen are not left out. They have also sacked people from their homes and overtaken their farmlands and dissipated communities. The frustrating dilemma is that not even a single individual has been arrested for prosecution, yet we have a government that claims to be for the people. Their ineptitude has rippling effects which include economic meltdown, institutional decay and social incoherence.

Given the apparent insecurity situation in Nigeria today, one doubts the place of the peoples' social and political majority. The people were robbed of that democratic right at the voting centers of the 2019 general elections by the presence of soldiers, who, instead of securing our national boarders from terrorists in the North-East, were all over the place 'securing' ballot boxes for the highest bidder. And the question is, to whose advantage? Of course, not in the interest of the people, but that of selfish politicians.

Our democracy is still at crossroads and the discourses for solutions seem to be stillborn. Part of the reason is that efforts made to involve the people in discussions on political affairs have often been swept under the carpet by demagogues in the guise of statesmen. This brings about a critical examination of the second part of my analysis of the place of the people within our democracy who should use their position "to conduct their own affairs". Do citizens of Nigeria really conduct their own affairs regarding their political life? A survey of the institutions meant to enhance the conduct of their affairs confirm my fears. The three arms of government are involved in a cold war that has crippled governance. Accusations of money laundering among office holders, and inability of government to bring perpetrators to book, the invasion of the National Assembly by security agents without recourse to due process, flagrant abuse of power and office by politicians, and worse still, intimidation of the *demos* by security agents, which impedes whatever efforts the people make toward conducting their own affairs. What of basic amenities like electricity, good roads and clean water? Their apparent lack has become the Golgotha on which the populace is nailed. Ojukwu decries the situation, observing that succeeding governments since independence have contrived to make Nigerians strangers in their land.[10]

The clamor to leave the country which is occasioned by insecurity at all levels corroborates Ojukwu's stand. It is a clear vote of no confidence on the government and the last hope to address the anomaly was the National Confab convoked by the immediate past President Goodluck Jonathan in 2014. Its recommendations were meant to address the plight of the people politically, socially and otherwise. It addressed national questions and recommended among other things true federalism: a system that would guarantee the freedom of the people, their economic and social empowerment, through agro-based competitive economy. But true to type, the unitary form of democracy run by military men in civilian clothes preferred the present status quo and its attendant sapping of the collective will of the people. Holding the people down has been their *modus operandi* but the lamentations of the people is of such intensity that it calls for attention.


## Redefining Nigerian Democracy

To redefine and redirect our democracy, the government as a matter of

---

[10] Emeka Odumegwu-Ojukwu, *Because I am Involved*, Ibadan, Spectrum Books, 1989, p.28.

urgency must restructure the country constitutionally. The present federal structure, to many, is no longer a viable option; it empowers the center to the detriment of component states. For a good number of Nigerians, the parliamentary system adopted at the dawn of independence seems to be a better option. It not only sustained unity amid our divergent nature, but also encouraged self-reliance and development among the regions. Such restructuring Anoje-Eke reiterates has to do with fundamental social and political reforms, socio-economic changes and geographical rearrangements.[11] Such rearrangement, democratically carried out, would guarantee a place for the people against the *status quo* which is an imposition from the military which does not represent the will of the people. Corroborating the will of the people in drafting a constitution, Udombana writes:

> A constitution cannot be foisted on a people, any more than one can force a marriage on two incompatible partners or take an unwilling horse to a river bank and force it to drink water. A people must mutually agree to live together and mutually agree on the terms of that compact before translating that agreement into a written code.[12]

In fairness to the people of Nigeria, they were not duly consulted in drafting the present constitutional structure imposed on them by military men. The post war effects that occasioned imbalance in military structure paved way for dominance of a group of people and consequently a privileged position in the Constitution. Such privileged positions with the attendant lopsided notions of justice, account for the civil strife that has become the order of the day. It has continued to spur the nation-wide clamor for restructuring, raising fundamental questions. Why is it that successive governments always seem to begin from the scratch fifty-nine (59) years after independence? Why the agitations for

---

[11] Anoje-Eke, A Nation at Cross-Roads, p. 53.

[12] Udombana, Nsongurua J., Constitutional Restructuring in Nigeria: An Impact Assessment (April 25, 2017). Available at SSRN: https://ssrn.com/abstract=2960030 or http://dx.doi.org/10.2139/ssrn.2960030

autonomy from ethnic groups like Movement for the Actualization of the Sovereign State of Biafra (MASSOB), Indigenous Peoples of Biafra (IPOB), the Yoruba Liberation Command (YOLICOM), Movement for the Survival of Ogoni People (MOSOP), Oodua People's Congress (OPC), Movement for the Emancipation of the Niger Delta (MEND), Niger Delta Movement (NDM), and so on? They point at feelings of injustice and neglect which are a major cause of revolution in regimes according to Aristotle.[13] Consequently, the support for restructuring from non-governmental groups like Southern Nigeria and Middle Belt Development Forum (SNMBDF), The United Action for Change, The South East Governors Forum, The Eastern Nigeria Governors Forum, The Catholic Bishops Conference of Nigeria, among others, lend legitimacy to the outcry for reshaping our present status as a country. If the status quo is not yielding the expected result, moves against restructuring are ones against the will of the people as documented in the 2014 draft of a sovereign national conference.

Response to the will of the people for restructuring would bring the desired change and not mere mantra as championed by the ruling party APC. It would address the greatest challenge facing democracy in Nigeria identified by Udenwagu as unwillingness of the political class to leave office. He argues that we have not had a change of governance since independence given the recycling of individuals or their cohorts to perpetuate themselves in office.[14] Their unwillingness to leave office is neither based on their good will for the people, the will of the people, nor their excellence in office. It is rather anchored on selfish interest evident in looting of our national treasury with the adverse effect of 'massive miseries in a land of massive wealth'. It alludes to a lack in our structure of governance – inefficiency, with its attendant consequences. There are no defined policies with infrastructural decay, lack of basic amenities, and industries to cushion the adverse effects of unemployment among the youth and worse still, the insensitivity of the present administration to address the issue – *Nemo dat quod non habet*. Yes, no one gives what he has not. They must bow to nature who

---

[13] Cfr. Aristotle, Politics, V, 2. 1302a 28-29.

[14] Kevin Udenwagu, "The Weakness of Democracy According to Aristotle: A Critical Study from the Point of View of Political Philosophy." Ph.D. Dissertation, Salesian Pontifical University, Rome, 2018, p. 76.

through the law of diminishing returns demands the exit of our current politicians from the political stage. There is need for a new breed of technocrats, with requisite ideas and the political will to move the nation forward.

In addition to restructuring, we need to uphold the rule of law in our constitution. The rule of law is 'the principle that all people and institutions are subject to and accountable to law that is fairly applied and enforced; the principle of government by law'. Part of the dilemma of our beloved nation is the impunity with which the government and its officials turn deaf ears to the rule of law. It makes a mess of the polity, leaving the citizens defenseless with irredeemable sense of apathy to governance. To uphold the rule of law, I suggest among other things, strict separation of the three arms of government to enable checks and balances. Regarding separation of powers among the three arms of government, I argue for Aristotle's stand based on common matters of public interest. His idea is not just one of separate spheres as we understand in contemporary politics, but one based on common matters. It implies therefore, that the common matters which concern the deliberative organ should also include some judicial matters, and the deliberative can itself be divided up among certain executive matters.[15] This kind of power check according to Aristotle will ensure that common matters of public interest meet the required standard. It will also ensure due process prior to passage of bills.

Furthermore, our educational policies should also be reviewed. For a sound educational curriculum aimed at achieving its desired end, we must revive our lost cultural values and make them the foundational basis of such curriculum. As such, we have something to transmit in the process of education described by Jaeger as the process by which a community preserves and transmits its physical [cultural] and intellectual character.[16] Lack of such foundational basis accounts for the instability of our educational system and consequently failure in governance. As a way out, our policy makers should incorporate in our curriculum democratic education in Aristotelian terms, 'education proper to a regime':

---

[15] Aristotle, Politics, IV,14. 1298a 1-3.

[16] Cfr. Werner Jaeger, Paideia. *The Ideals of Greek Culture*, Vol. 1, tr. Gilbert Highet, New York, Oxford University Press, 1945, p. xiii.

> But the greatest of all the things that have been
> mentioned with a view to making regimes lasting –
> though it is now slighted by all – is education relative
> to the regimes. For there is no benefit in the most
> beneficial laws, even when these have been approved by
> all those engaging in politics, if they are not going to
> be habituated and educated in the regime.[17]

The importance of education in achieving stability in governance is underlined by Aristotle's insistence on proper education for the citizens. Regarding his type of education – relative to particular regimes – he meant that citizens should be trained not to recognize specific claims to justice of their particular constitution, but to adapt among them the competing claims to justice especially by opposing factions. Lack of democratic education and its attendant justice (or injustice/corrupt justice system) has been the bane of Nigerian democracy. Such justice recognizes constructive criticisms and submissions from opposition parties. But in our context in Nigeria, ruling parties have lopsided notions of justice to the extent that party constitution is used in place of national constitution and opposition parties regarded as enemies. We should educate the citizens and politicians as well to understand and incorporate competing claims to justice for stability in governance.

**Conclusion**

This paper addresses the problem of democracy in Nigeria. Given the apparent weakness of our democratic regimes, past and present, evident in a total system collapse, this paper points out part of the problems with suggestive measures. The paper acknowledges the weak nature of our democracy, evident in our wrong understanding, interpretation and application of the term democracy and its attendant principle of freedom. Understood as government of the people, by the people and for the people, one doubts our understanding of the real meaning of democracy given our interpretation and implementation of that term. Democracy well understood and adapted within a political community,

---

[17] Aristotle, Politics, V, 9. 1310a 13-17.

questions the place of the people within the confines of its application. However, our wrong interpretation of democracy is based on a misunderstanding of the principle of freedom on which democratic principles stand. The consequence is enormous – a democracy at crossroads.

Analyzing the state of the nation democratically, we identified military intervention in Nigerian politics as part of our undoing. They not only disrupted democratic governance but also laid foundation for impunity given their ineptitude in governance. Civilians/politicians also have their share of the blame. We pointed out that under civilians, we can at least boast of running a democratic system of government and elections conducted for elective posts. However, using Maritain's definition of democracy as yardstick for measurement, we also fault our politicians for not living above board; marred electoral processes, looting of national treasury, poor infrastructure, insecurity, and crime occasioned by joblessness among the youth are part of the issues begging for question.

As a way out, this paper suggested constitutional restructuring as a major step onto redefining our democratic structure. This will not only afford the people an opportunity of saying their mind in matters concerning the affairs of their political society but will also address the lopsided sense of justice which according to Aristotle, is a trigger of revolution. Among other things, our educational policies should be reviewed to enhance proper education aimed at transmission of worthwhile values. The rule of law should also be upheld. There should be a review of the appointment of the chief Judge of the federation to enhance the independence of the judiciary and respect of court injunctions by government officials. These will not only restore the confidence of the people but will also ensure stability of governance. Such stability occasioned by the rule of law ensures that power is sustained by structures of governance against the status quo where individuals take over power and wield it arbitrarily without recourse to existing structures – dictatorship. On another note, the paper recommends a reform of Nigerian electoral process. The chairman of the electoral body should not be appointed by the president to avoid the ugly scenario of 'he that pays the piper' dictating the tune. The electoral body should also be independent of the arms of government, not only in name but also in action. This is unlike one sees in the character of our present electoral body in Nigeria– the Independent National Electoral Commission (INEC).

# Chapter 3

# Money Politics in Nigeria

Cletus Umezinwa

## Introduction

Generally, there are some people whose two objects of love in a civil society are: power and wealth. Depending on the prevailing situation, some love power and appropriate it to acquire wealth. The converse is also true, that some hanker after and amass wealth to acquire power. In politics, however, it appears that the number of people seeking political power to acquire wealth outnumbers those that acquire wealth as a means to aspire to power. With the benefit of hindsight, one can affirm that this is true of Nigeria. And this has contributed to a large extent to her failure as a state.

Some writers reflecting on Nigeria as a failed state have pointed out a number of factors that have contributed inexorably to her miserable failure. Such factors include ethnic chauvinism, religious bigotry, bad leadership, cancerous corruption, etc. Various solutions have been proffered as a way out of the doldrums. This paper argues that the bane of Nigeria's failure is money politics. And that the solution lies in putting in place a political arrangement that would prevent people from enriching themselves from public trust. This claim is made because politics appears to be the easiest and quickest way to become rich in the country. Chinua Achebe states in his book *There Was A Country* that the World Bank "released numbers indicating that about $400 Billion has been pilfered from Nigeria's treasury since independence."[18] This, of course, does not include other areas through which political office holders enrich themselves. All loopholes, therefore, need to be closed and buttons properly tightened to halt this trend of making money unjustly out of office.

---

[18]C. Achebe, *There Was A Country*, Penguin Group: England, 2012, p. 249.

The money politics brings about a topsy-turvy situation where a few are rich but the many are poor. The middle class is hardly recognisable. To address this problem squarely, a political arrangement that should lead to a remarkable increase in the size of the middle class and the extreme reduction of the upper and lower classes ought to be put in place. This is what we are essentially proposing. To do this effectively this paper considers theoretically the advantages of having the middle class in the polity. It will go on to argue that a political arrangement that promotes a rapid expansion of the middle is suitable for Nigeria. It will insist that theoretically any political practice that favours some over others is against the idea of state formation. It will make practical suggestions on how to remove the obstacles lying on the way of reframing the constitution to stimulate increase in the number of the middle class.

**Aristotle on the Theoretical Benefits of the Middle Class**
We wish to use Aristotle to highlight the advantages of the middle class in the polity. In his study of the existing constitutions of his time, Aristotle observes that there are three main constitutions, namely, monarchy, aristocracy and timocracy. These are good constitutions. They are good because the leaders govern not for their interests but for the welfare of their subjects. The difference between the constitutions is that monarchy is a government of one person, aristocracy by a few and timocracy by many. The perverse forms of these constitutions are tyranny, oligarchy and democracy. What these bad constitutions have in common is that the leaders govern for their personal interests and not for those of their subjects. In sum, there are six kinds of constitution. In his *Nicomachean Ethics*, Aristotle shows that these six forms of government are analogically related with the family relationships.[19] Monarchy resembles where the father rules with paternal love whereas in tyranny he rules like a master over his slaves. Aristocracy is similar to where the husband and wife govern together, each carrying out the duty where he or she has the competence whereas in oligarchy either the husband or wife dominates and does not assign appropriate roles to the other. Timocracy is like the relationship between brothers while democracy is like a household without a master.

On a practical note, Aristotle calls for a mixed form of constitution

---

[19]Aristotle, Nicomachean Ethics, VIII, x, 1160b, 4.

consisting of oligarchy and democracy. This is because the oligarchs and the democrats are mortal enemies embroiled in bitter rivalries that make socio-political development a mirage. He calls for this mixed form of constitution in attempt to harmonise the interests of the wealthy (oligarchs) and the poor (democrats) as well as remove the limitations existing in both forms of government. Part of the limitations is that when, for example, the government in power is oligarchy, the wealthy few who run the government exhibit insolence and contempt. And if the form of government in power is democracy, the poor who are in the majority in this system of government exhibit malice and covet the wealth or the position of the rich. In either system of government developmental progress is hampered. This is the reason behind Aristotle's call for a mixed form of constitution consisting of oligarchy and democracy. This form of mixed constitution is what he calls constitutional government.

In the constitutional government as well as in other forms of constitution there are three classes of people, the extraordinarily rich, the very poor and the middle class. For Aristotle, virtue stands in the middle; it is the mean between two extremes of deficiency and excess. This is a conviction he espoused in the *Nicomachean Ethics* in his discussion on virtue.[20] In his *Politics* he subscribes to the same idea of adopting the middle course between two extremes.[21] The mean is virtuous and the extremes are vicious. This is why he prefers constitutional government because it is the mean between oligarchy and democracy. He prefers this for a number of reasons. First, it has the potential of reducing tensions arising from insolence, malice and covetousness existing in the polity. Second it promotes the attainment of public good. Third, its adoption as a policy will lead to increase in the number of people in the middle class. Fourth, it will reduce to the barest minimum the number of the very rich and the very poor.

Now when the people in the middle class outnumber the other two classes; and when these hold power, there is significant reduction of impunity, there is more respect for the laws provided in the constitution. But the very rich are impudent and insolent; impunity holds sway in their case if they are in government. They are not ready

---

[20] Aristotle, Nicomachean Ethics, II, vi, 1106b, 12-14.

[21] Aristotle, Politics, IV, ix, 1295a, 2.

to be under any authority or obey the laws or respect the constitution. On the other hand, the poor who are subservient to authority are not familiar with the intricacies of the acts of governance. And so, in constitutional governments, these negative features of oligarchy and democracy are eliminated. According to Aristotle, the citizens in the middle class "have the greatest security in the states; for they do not themselves covet other men's good as the poor do, nor do the other classes covet their substance as the poor covet that of the rich; and because they are neither plotted against nor plotting they live free from danger."[22] Besides, the equality of citizens which the state aims at is mostly guaranteed where the middle class is numerous. The dominant presence of the middle class minimises frictions and party factions. In a system of government in which there is dominance of the middle class there is not only significant reduction of impunity, impudence, insolence, malice, covetousness, but there is also respect for the rule of law. When these are in place, money politics will fizzle out and will exist only in name and not in fact.

**Mixed Constitution Suitable for Nigeria**
Many of the forms of constitution enumerated by Aristotle are domiciled in Nigeria. There were about 250 ethnic groups in Nigeria in 1914. They were in existence with their respective forms of government before their merger in Nigeria. Ever since, the major ethnic groups have been the Hausa, the Yoruba and the Igbo. The Hausa are said to be oligarchic, the Yoruba aristocratic and the Igbo democratic. Because the ethnic groups were forcefully brought to exist together as one entity there has been problem of cohesion and integration. This problem has snowballed over the years creating a yawning gap between the rich and the poor. The rich are getting richer and the poor getting poorer. About 100 Nigerians own private jets which they use over N30 billion to maintain annually.[23] And yet Nigeria is the world capital of poverty. About 87 million Nigerians live in abject poverty of less than 1.90 dollar a day. The external reserve is depleting. A large part of it is being used to stabilize the Naira. The external reserve stands at $45 billion while external debt is about $65 billion.

---

[22]Aristotle, Politics, IV, ix, 1295b, 7

[23] www.hotvibesmedia.com.ng

Nigeria uses 30% of its budget which is about N5 trillion to service external debts. The current rate of inflation is 12%. Unemployment varies by age group. Youth unemployment is above 60%. General unemployment of persons between sixteen and sixty-four stands officially at 24%.[24] There is need to enact laws that would bring about not only national cohesion and integration (mixed constitution) but also national development. This is achievable if these laws aim at the dominance of the middle class in the polity. To this end, there is need to adopt a strategic policy that aims at the increase of the middle class.

**Increasing the Middle Class in Nigeria**

How to increase the number of people in the middle class is to empower the citizens financially with grants to finance their education and lend them money to begin their private businesses, a policy if properly executed can lead to a less importation of certain products and encourage the exportation of others. But this policy can only be promoted if the government has enough resources. And for government to have sufficient resources to fulfil its obligation there is need to have appropriate tax regime, have other sources of income apart from oil and then close conduit pipes through which country's money get into private pockets. To this effect, we make the following proposals:

1. **Appropriate Tax Regime.** There are some Nigerian politicians and businessmen that are extremely rich. Their lifestyle is ethereal. Some fly private jets as already noted. The sources of income of these wealthy Nigerians ought to be discovered. They should be asked to make tax contributions above those of the middle class and low-income earners. This idea will help not only to improve the national revenue but will also whittle down their influence to use money to sponsor thugs to bring wrong people into political office.

2. **Closing Leakages**

a. **National Assembly.** The former governor of the Central Bank of Nigeria, Lamido Sanusi said in 2010 that 25% of the total overhead costs of government is spent on the National Assembly. This is

---

[24] The above financial figures are courtesy of renowned economist Prof. H. Ichoku, 2019.

outrageous. But the uproar that greeted the revelation has petered out without concrete action taken to address the anomaly. The National Assembly is made up of 109 senators and 360 members of the House of Representatives. The amount allocated to them is gargantuan. This is the reason why so many aspire to join the National Assembly. This is a place to make money with greatest ease. The salaries and allowances of the members are yet to be reviewed by the Revenue Mobilisation, Allocation and Fiscal Commission. They are sacred cows. And so, a law ought to be enacted to empower the Revenue Mobilisation, Allocation and Fiscal Commission to review their salaries, allowances, pension and gratuities to be in line with other government workers and economic realities of the nation. It has been observed that the salaries and allowances of the Nigerian legislators are among the highest in the world. Senator Shehu Sani revealed in 2018 that each senator receives 700,000 Naira as salary and allowances, 13.5 million Naira as running cost. Besides these, there is 200 million Naira constituency funds given to government agency on behalf of each senator for the execution of projects in their localities[25].

b. **Pension and Gratuities**. It is the practice in Nigeria that former governors aspire and get elected to the National Assembly. They receive pension as former governors and then salaries, allowances and running costs as members of the National Assembly. This practice is outrageous and a betrayal of gross insensitivity to the plight of the average Nigerian. A law ought to be enacted for the political office holders to receive one emolument at a time.

c. **Passing of Bills**. There ought to be a law that makes it criminal for the President or the governors to give financial rewards to the legislators whenever they pass a bill. Why should they be given extra reward for doing something for which they were elected? But where do the Presidents and governors get the money which they use to reward the legislators? Is this money in the budget or is there a misdirection of fund meant for capital projects?

---

[25] https://www.premiumtimesng.com/news/headlines/261085-confirmed-nigerian-senators-receive-n13-5-million-monthly-apart-from-salaries.html

**d. Security Vote**. Both at the state and federal levels, there is what is called security vote. This is the fund designed to be used to provide security at the state and federal government levels. The President or the governor releases the fund for above projects at his discretion. But one thing that characterises this fund is that it is not accounted for. There is need for a legislation that demands transparency and proper accountability on how such a fund is dispensed.

**e. Constituency Fund**. This is the money allocated for development projects in the constituencies of the legislators. Efforts should be made to ensure that such funds are not misdirected. A committee of religious leaders, town unions and NGOs should be constituted at various levels of government to ensure that the money is properly used for the designated projects.

**f. Oil Blocks.** Licences to oil blocks owners ought to be revoked. Large sums of money accruing to the government are lost through the policy of oil blocks. Surely any attempt by any government to revoke it will meet stiff opposition from the beneficiaries of the policy. But that should not be a reason not to fight fiercely for its abrogation.

**g. Feeding Policy.** Government's policy of feeding pupils in the primary schools ought to be abolished. This policy is aimed at encouraging pupils to develop interest in education. It is, however, reported that some pupils attend the school and take their portion of food and disappear. The huge sums of money being spent on school feeding programs can be saved and used as grants to people to improve the agricultural products or their businesses.

The points noted above (**a-g**) and proposals made therefrom are necessary if Nigeria is to minimise the existence of money politics which is a shibboleth in many developed countries of the world. But the ineradicable fact, however, is that many of the beneficiaries of the money politics will not be disposed to adopt policies that will affect them adversely. They will invent arguments, albeit flabby and shabby, to enfeeble any measure that would lead to a radical reduction or total elimination of what they illegally accumulate for themselves. Nigeria has carried out several constitutional conferences but not one was signed into law. They were exercises in futility. Billions of Naira invested in the national conversation simply went down the drain without much fuss. The loss of the humongous amount of money meant nothing to those who failed to implement them.

There are some people who call for revolution. They rely on the saying that those who fail to make peaceful change possible, make violent change inevitable. Well, this saying may have meaning and validity outside Nigeria. The strong ethnic affiliation in Nigeria will not allow it to work. There were in recent times, political insurrections in Tunisia, Egypt, Sudan etc. Earlier, countries like France, Britain, U.S., Germany, Russia, etc had reacted against their leaders. But they emerged stronger from such rebellions. These cannot be replicated in Nigeria because of entrenched ethnic interest. It is better to seek other feasible alternatives that would lead to a strategic implementation of the proposals that would lead ultimately to increase of the middle class. But before this, it would be necessary to examine theoretically why money politics is a contradiction to the intent and purpose of state formation, why it is albatross to development. The aim is to urge those who oppose the elimination of the money politics to see reason and reconsider their stand.

**Money Politics against the Objective of State Formation**
The political philosophy of John Locke influenced tremendously the framers of the constitutions of America and Britain.[26] Nigeria is practising a Presidential system of government akin to America. And so, it is appropriate to use John Locke's political philosophy to point out why money politics contradicts the aim of civil society. The reason is because money politics creates political morass that engenders huge gap between the rich and the poor, the haves and have nots; it makes the rich get richer and the poor poorer. It eliminates the middle class while empowering financially those in the political class.

John Locke in his political theory made a hypothetical distinction between the state of nature and civil society. His state of nature, like that of Thomas Hobbes, is acephalous, no king, no government. But it is guided by the law of nature. In this state, all are equal because

---

[26] J. Omoregbe, *A Simplified History of Western Philosophy*, Vol. 2, Ikeja: Joja Educational Research and Publishers Limited, 2003, p. 66.

they are all created by God, they belong to the same species, they have the same faculty and the same advantages of nature. Because all are equal on the basis of the aforementioned reasons, they are independent and free. And no one has the right, therefore, to subjugate anyone or violate his or her freedom. Locke says that the law of nature that guides the action in the state of nature succinctly states that "being all equal and independent, no one ought to harm another in his life, health, liberty, or possessions."[27]

Now to ensure that harm is done to no one and that the liberty of the individual is respected, the law of nature entrusts the punishment of violators into the hands of the individuals. Everyone has the right to exact punishment on whomsoever injures him. The punishment, however, is not to be dished out arbitrarily. It must be done with two aims in mind: reparation and deterrence. The aggressor has to make reparation for the damage he caused. And the punishment ought to serve as deterrent to would-be offenders. Locke points out that in carrying out these two aims, the punishment should be proportional to the offence committed.

Locke, however, notes that there are inconveniences in the state of nature. The first is that the individual is a judge in his own case. The second is that in a fit of anger and passion, the injured party may unleash punishment on the aggressor that is much more than the offence he committed. Thirdly, there are certain occasions when the injured party cannot even obtain justice because the aggressor is physically stronger than him. In order to offset these inconveniences that affect the full implementation of one's liberty, Locke says, "God hath certainly appointed government to restrain the partiality and violence of men. I easily grant that civil government is the proper remedy for the inconveniences of the state of nature…since 'tis easy to be imagined that he who was so unjust as to do his brother an injury, will scarcely be so just as to condemn himself for it."[28] The formation of civil society is therefore an imperative.

A civil society is one in which there is the legislature entrusted with the making of laws and the executive that enforces them. Both derive their

---

[27] John Locke, *Of Civil Government and Toleration*, London: Cassel and Company Limited, 1905, p. 11.

[28] John Locke, ibid., p. 15.

authority from the individuals. They come together and give their consent to or submit their liberty to protect their property to a person or group of persons. They empower them to use their collective consent to make laws and enforce them on their behalf for the safety of their property. In making the laws, the lawgivers ought to be guided by the law of nature. They should enact laws which promote the liberties and protect the property which the individuals had in the state of nature and not laws which deny them their liberties and make them poorer than they were in the hypothetical state of nature. When they make laws that suit their own comfort and fancy, they miss *the raison d'être* for their establishment; they empower themselves financially and short-change the subjects who have given them the sacred trust over their property. For Locke, the legislative power "is limited to the public good of the society. It is a power that hath no other end but the preservation, and therefore can never have a right to destroy, enslave, or designedly to impoverish the subjects."[29] The legislators do not have more powers than the individuals had in the state of nature. The power was given for protection and not for destruction.

Locke acknowledges that the leaders who work for the people should be rewarded. But he added that it is not their duty to fix their own reward. It is the people themselves who gave them this assignment that ought to do so. As he puts it: "'Tis true governments cannot be supported without great charge, and it is fit everyone who enjoys a share of the protection should pay out of his estate his proportion for the maintenance of it. But still it must be with his own consent."[30]

There are two outstanding lessons from Locke vis-à-vis the political situation in Nigeria. The first is that the individuals are not to be disadvantaged because they entered into civil society. They are not to be made poorer than they would otherwise be if they were not in organised government. The second point is that the leaders are not the ones to determine their emoluments. It is the function of the citizens to do so. This is in contradiction to what is obtainable in Nigeria where the National Assembly members determine their "running cost" or state assemblies fix life pension and other outrageous goodies for the ex-governors and their deputies. As the Nigeria leaders may not be willing to abide by the theoretical

---

[29] John Locke, ibid., p. 81.

[30] John Locke, ibid., p. 85.

admonitions of John Locke, there is need to have a national dialogue in which things like money politics, emoluments, the proposals listed above **(a-g)** etc. are to be discussed.

## National Dialogue

Karl Popper in his political philosophy advocates for what he calls piece meal social engineering. He is against total overhaul of any political system in a bid to achieve happiness in an ideal state. For him the work of a social engineer is not to achieve happiness but eliminate suffering and pain in the society. He believes that the reasonable and practicable thing in a polity is to identify problems and eliminate them as they arise. This is easier to achieve than to attain ideal state and happiness.[31] Ideal state is figment of the imagination, it is will-o'-the-wisp.

Money politics is a corrosive phenomenon that hamstrings development. It is a terrible problem. And since leaders are not ready and willing to deal with it decisively, a national dialogue becomes an option. Of course, national dialogues had been held in the past without success. Part of the reason for the failure is because the people were not carried along. It is the people that give their consent to their leaders. When these leaders derail from the mandate given to them, the same people need to come together and state in clear terms the policies that would ensure that they are not disadvantaged in the civil society. They do this in a National Conference in which people from all walks of life participate in a representative basis to proffer solutions to identifiable problems. For the deliberations to move smoothly and successfully we must note that "Discourses take place in particular social contexts and are subject to limitations of time and place…Topics and contributions have to be organized. The adjournment, and resumption of discussions must be arranged. Because of these factors, institutional measures are needed to sufficiently neutralize empirical limitations and avoidable internal and external interference so that the idealized conditions always already presupposed by participants in argumentation can at least be adequately approximated."[32]

---

[31] Karl Popper, *The Open Society and its Enemies*, vol. 1, London: George Routledge, 1947, p. 139-140.

[32] Jürgen Habermas, *Moral Consciousness and Communicative Action*, Cambridge: Polity Press, 2007, 92.

The main problem of the National Conference usually begins after the resolutions have been adopted by majority of the members. The resolutions are given to the National Assembly for further deliberations. They may tinker on some of the documents. They submit the final copies thereafter to the President for his ascent. In this arrangement, the National Assembly or the President may reject or even moderate the resolutions particularly if they do not favour them.

But this is wrong. It is not proper to send the resolutions to the National Assembly or the President. If the members of the National Assembly had been able to enact laws that affect the people positively there would not have been any need to convoke the National Conference in the first place. The President and the National Assembly are more likely to insist on those points that in actual fact led to the calls for National Conference.

To pass the resolutions of the National Conference into law, there is need to call for a referendum. This should be done after months of sensitization on the contents of the resolutions. This is more reasonable since the executive and the legislature have failed in the sacred trust given to them to make justifiable positive laws. The people ought now to assert their rights directly on how they are to be governed. If the result of the referendum is positive, then the resolutions become laws. But it is more likely to be positive than negative for the participants at the conference will be at the vanguard for their passage.

## Conclusion

If the government has the will to adopt the above recommendations, it will have enough resources to execute its recurrent and capital expenditure. It will also have enough money to grant loans to people, an action which has the potential of increasing the middle class and reducing the number of the very rich and the very poor. And when there is the dominance of the middle class, and the government in power is made up of those in the middle class, then the country will begin to witness less impunity in government, more respect for the constitution and rule of law, and massive national development.

# Chapter 4

# Revolution of Minds in the Nigeria Project: The Socratic Paradigm

M. Nkechi Ezeanyino

## Introduction: The Nigeria of Our Day

It takes perhaps only a blind and deaf person to claim ignorance of the situation of the Nigerian Society today. To say that the Society is that in which almost nothing works will be an understatement. For instance, the security situation in the Country has so deteriorated that people are living in constant fear. It has been alleged that one Senator of the Federal Republic from the Northern part of the Country travels to his hometown in a rickety type of car to evade kidnappers, and another one resorted to travelling in an ambulance. It is not a secret that Abuja-Kaduna road is a haven for kidnappers and armed robbers. Thanks to the recent rail transport from Abuja to Kaduna, people could now travel that axis in relative peace. It is equally true that many prominent people rarely travel to their villages for security reasons. These are just a few examples, because it will be dumbfounding if people narrate all the tactics they employ to secure and protect themselves in this present age. The systematic program of the Fulani herdsmen to exterminate the indigenous people in parts of the Country, at times disguised as armed bandits, is another security issue that gives people great course for concern. This issue of security has scared many investors causing them to withdraw from Nigeria, while intending investors are apprehensive. This has affected our economy very adversely.

Our healthcare facilities are in many cases moribund with little or no equipments, hence the haves resort to overseas healthcare. Our educational system is decaying in leaps and bounds, with the incessant industrial actions by academic staff due to lack of adequate funding and infrastructure in government institutions. The medics and paramedics are not left out in the incessant industrial actions. Electricity supply is very often epileptic thereby affecting our economy negatively. Do we talk of ethnic and religious bigotry and lack of mutual trust or rather mutual suspicion among the various ethnic groups in the country, the frequent warnings against, and efforts at discouraging hate speech notwithstanding? Ours is a Society that thrives on lies especially from the powers that be. Lying seems to have become part and parcel of the official instruments of governance, with the effect that citizens are often left in the dark as to the true situation of things. Who then can be trusted?

The situation is such that has nourished the sense of despair in the minds of many Nigerians even among the intellectuals that they seem to believe that the situation is irredeemable. This is particularly with regard to institutionalized corruption which has eaten deep into the fabrics of most Nigerians, children and youths inclusive. For most Nigerians, there cannot be any "success" in life but by means of corrupt practices. And so life has become survival of the fittest if one has to make his mark in the Society where money rather than good name is seen as the utmost value.

What of crime in all its ramifications, – armed robbery, kidnapping, rapes, "419" et cetera – the offshoot of a very corrupt Society? The number of unemployed youths roaming the streets is on the increase. The situation has given rise to frequent cases of suicide almost on a daily basis. A Clinical Psychologist blamed the rising cases of suicide *"on the deplorable conditions in our society which he said have adversely affected people's health. He bemoaned the amount of violence, poverty and suffering Nigerians face on daily basis"*.[33] Respect for rule of law seems now to be "an essential commodity" that even some in government could violate the Constitution without qualms, and it will be swept under the carpet. Hence the law seems to be made only for the common person.

What a gory picture of the Nigerian Society painted here. In a situation like this, what do we do? How can we reclaim the Nigerian Society to count once again among the civilized Societies? This is the aim of this write-up based on the retraining of mentality – re-orientation

---

[33] Fr. Anthony Aneke, Chikezie Ogbonna & Njideka Eze, "More Reasons Why People Commit Suicide in Nigeria – Psyche Expert Explains" in *The Choice Flame*, Volume 9, No 14. Mid June, 2019, p. 10.

of values. There is need for real mental revolution of the citizenry especially that of the young population. It is all about grooming, from the grassroots, a new breed of Nigerians who could stand on their two feet, think objectively and so be able to organize this Country in such a way that every citizen will have a sense of belonging, and the Country will equally count once again among the committee of Nations.

We need however to see what past and present governments have done and are still doing toward this mental re-orientation, in a bid to ameliorating this pitiable condition of our beloved Nation. Thereafter, we present our own proposal for achieving this purpose, and then make our submission as a conclusion.

**Past Efforts Towards This Mental Revolution:**
It is worthy of note that some past governments realized the need for this re-orientation of the minds of her citizens, and in consequence initiated some programs to that effect. Such programs like **"Mass Mobilization for Self-Reliance, Social Justice and Economic Recovery (MAMSER)"**, and **"War Against Indiscipline (WAI)"** readily come to mind. The War Against Indiscipline, which became very popular during the military regime of His Excellency Mohammadu Buhari and Idiagbo, seemed to have somehow affected people's mentality and life but later died a natural death, just like the others which fizzled out with the end of the regime that started them. During that time, people could at least behave with discipline.

The most recent of the programs – **"Re-Branding Nigeria: Nigeria Good People Great Nation"** – the brain-child of the Late former Minister of Information and Communication, Prof. (Mrs.) Dora Nkem Akunyili,[34] was launched and the Logo unveiled in Abuja on Tuesday, March 17, 2009. It was said that the campaign attracted *"several prominent Nigerians and members of the civil Society, organized labor, private sector and students, who took turns in expressing their hope for a better Nigeria and their desire for a corrupt-free Nigeria"* and *"one that guarantees individual rights and liberties".*[35] The caliber of the people at the

---

[34] Late Prof. (Mrs.) Dora Nkem Akunyili served under President Umaru Musa Yaradua and his Vice Goodluck Ebele Jonathan.

[35] Uche Nworah, "Nigeria Unveils 'Good People Great Nation' Rebranding Campaign", Abuja, March 17, 2009.

campaign and their contributions were indications of how Nigerians feel about the Nigeria Society. It was then constantly used as a jingle, "Nigeria Good People Great Nation".

The present Government of **"Change"** of President Muhammadu Buhari in its bid at fighting corruption devised the slogan **"Change Begins with Me"** and later added the program of **"Whistle Blowing"** which encouraged people to report corrupt individuals or organizations to the "Economic and Financial Crimes Commission (EFCC) for adequate action. The Federal Radio Corporation of Nigeria (FRCN) is not left out in this effort of re-orientating the minds of Nigerians to a morally, better behavior, through its numerous programs.[36]

All these efforts notwithstanding, it seems that the situation is deteriorating in leaps and bounds. This has led to near despair for many a Nigerian. What then do we do? Give in to despair or continue trying? We have resorted to the second option – to keep trying, hence our effort to introduce a method of education different from the normal ones, though it is an old method used in traditional Societies to inculcate morals and traditions on the young ones.

We have suggested before now, compulsory inclusion of core Philosophical Courses in our Tertiary Institutions irrespective of one's area of study, and induction course on the said philosophical courses for our elected leaders for the right development of their minds, to enhance development in other spheres of human endeavor. After all, it was the view of an ancient philosopher Aristotle, that only Philosopher-Kings (those young men and women groomed in Philosophy) are qualified to direct the affairs of the Nation as befits human beings. It is our contention that right mindset and orientation will make human choices and actions properly human and worthy of the human person[37]. This time around, we are considering the re-orientation of the minds of the young generation, the leaders of tomorrow. This is to equip them for the building of a

---

[36] Cf. Radio Nigeria Program: "Nigeria Go Betta" - Reconstruction of Moral Values. Monday, 28 November, 2011.

[37] Rev. Sr. (Dr.) Nkechi Ezeanyino, D.D.L., "*Philosophy, Value and Human Development*: A Panacea for Misplaced Priorities" in Cletus Umezinwa, Ed., Philosophical Essays on Human Problems. Nigeria: Afro-Orbit Publications Limited, 2013, pp. 145-146.

new Society in which integrity, truth, honesty, justice, love, patriotism, et cetera, will be seen and lived as true values. This will be achieved by giving them the type of education that can stimulate and develop their mental and moral growth.[38] Education worthy of the name should aim at producing sound and effective members of the Society. Simply put, we need a proper method of education that will prepare them for the building of a Society where God and human beings will be given their respective proper places. Hence the need to begin from the Primary, and even Nursery school level using this method. What is this method? It is what we call **"The Socratic Method"**.

**THE SOCRATIC METHOD:** All the controversy surrounding the person and teaching of Socrates notwithstanding, our main concern is on the man who is principally interested in ethical issues, meaning to raise human beings of excellent character.[39] According to Copleston, *"Socrates was deeply convinced of the value of the soul, in the sense of the thinking and willing subject, and he saw clearly the importance of knowledge, of true wisdom, if the soul is to be properly tended. What are the true values of human life which have to be realized in conduct?".*[40] He therefore devised a method of dialectic which he himself called "midwifery – maieutics" through which he elicits definition of ethical concepts from his interlocutors with the intention *"of getting others to produce true ideas in their minds, with a view to right action".*[41] For Socrates *"the chief goodness consists in the caring of the soul concerned with moral truth and moral understanding"*, that *"wealth does not bring goodness, but goodness brings wealth and every other blessing, both to the individual and to the*

---

[38] C.f. Sr. Dr. Nkechi Ezeanyino, DDL, "Being Learned or Being Educated? A Critical Question. Inaugural Lecture delivered on the 4th of October, 2008, at Bigard Memorial Seminary, Enugu" in Benjamin Ike Ewelu, Editor, *Philosophical Reflections on African Issues*. Enugu, Nigeria: Delta Publications (Nigerian) Limited, 2010, p. 2.

[39] Cf. Aristotle, Metaphysics A 987 b 1-3, M 1078 b 17-19.

[40] Frederick Copleston. *A History of Philosophy*, Vol. 1, Greece and Rome. London, New York: Continuum, Reprinted 2006, p. 107.

[41] Ibid.

*State*" and that *"life without examination (...) is not worth living".*[42] For Enoch Stumpf, *"The interior of man, said Socrates, is the seat of a unique activity, the activity of knowing, which leads to the practical activity of doing".*[43] This is the dialectic skill that will elicit from young minds searching questions with regard to customs in moral, religious and political behavior.[44]

This is a method in the *"form of cooperative argumentative dialogue between individuals, based on asking and answering questions to stimulate critical thinking and to draw out ideas and underlying presuppositions".*[45] Here participants will form what is known as "Socratic Circle or Seminar" where texts or concepts are systematically examined through questions and answers thereby elucidating already held beliefs to arrive at a deeper understanding of the text. The text will be given to the participants earlier, and on coming together, their aim is to work together to make out a better meaning of the text. No particular participant wins or loses the argument. The work of the teacher is that of moderating the discussion to see that the group keeps on the track. Here lies the significant difference between this method and most of the typical classroom methods which hitherto encourages memorization and one to one rendering of the memorized texts whether they make sense to the one who memorized them or not. While the students lead the questioning and discussion, the teacher is only the moderator. This in a sense could be called democratic method of education which is glaringly lacking in our present system of education. *"This approach is based on the belief that participants seek and gain deeper understanding of concepts in the text through thoughtful dialogue rather than memorizing information that has been provided for them. No matter what structure the teacher employs, the basic premise of the Seminar/Circle is to turn partial control and direction of the classroom over to the students. The Seminars encourage students to work together, creating*

---

[42] https://en.wikipedia.org/wiki/Socratic_Method.

[43] Samuel Enoch Stumpf, *Philosophy: History and Problems.* New York: McGraw-Hill Book Company, 1977, p. 39.

[44] Cf. Samuel Enoch Stumpf, Philosophy: History and Problems. Op. Cit., p. 46.

[45] Ibid.

*meaning from the text and to stay away from trying to find a correct interpretation. The emphasis is on critical and creative thinking".*[46]

Of the known teaching methods, it is the Discussion or Conversation Method that approximates to this Socratic Method. In the Discussion Method, the teacher brings out different familiar things and engages the pupils in discussing them. *"If properly directed, the method trains pupils to think well. The function of discussion is to weigh and consider facts, to determine its importance with reference to a certain purpose, to organize the facts with a view to their relation to a problem, to accept or reject them based on their worthwhileness or otherwise. Discussion gives opportunity to judge what is considered valuable or useless".*[47] Igboabuchi and Azubuike elaborated the different methods of teaching in Chapter 8 of their book. There is no gainsaying the fact that when people can, by themselves, critically analyze and find out the true nature of things and situations, thereby being convinced of their findings, they will surely behave according to good conscience. Institutionalized corruption, bad governance and their attendant woes, for example, could be reduced to the barest minimum, if not completely remedied. The method is meant to help people get in touch with reality and begin to think and behave like human beings who are truly rational.

**OUR SUBMISSION:** It is our honest submission that if the mentality of the young Nigerians is to be re-orientated, part of our educational methods has to change radically. To that effect, we suggest this Socratic Method to groom from the grassroots, our young minds to right thinking, right understanding and right conduct. There is no gainsaying the fact that most people live and die for what they believe in, Socrates being a typical example. Our personal experience of disciplining small and young children bears testimony to this. For example, if a small child did something wrong that deserves flogging, you will first of all elicit the nature of the act from the child, that is, if it thinks that the act is good or bad. If it acknowledges the wrongness of the act, or if it does not know, you will explain to the child why the act is bad before punishing it. Having clearly understood the reason for the punishment, it will henceforth desist from committing such act in the future. From questions and answers, one elicits the reason for the

---

[46] Wikipedia, op. cit.

[47] Benjamin O. Igboabuchi, Ph. D. and Ken Ayo Azubuike, M. Ed., *Childhood Education in Nigeria: An Introduction.* Onitsha, Nigeria: Lincel Publishers, 2006, pp. 116-117.

disciplinary measure from the child, thereby putting an end to further commission of the bad act, or at least the gradual reduction of the frequency of the commission. Good understanding leads to good action.

In order to achieve this, teachers have to be groomed in this method. We suggest the inclusion of Socrates and the Socratic Method in the Curriculum of our Teacher Education. This should be made compulsory subject and not elective. When they must have been groomed in this method, then they will start with Citizenship or Civic Education, the education aimed at building *"morally sound and upright citizens who would ensure the promotion of political and socio-economic development of Nigeria"*.[48] This education has to start from Nursery at their own level, through Primary, Secondary and Tertiary levels. If the mentality of the future generation, who is the hope of every Society, is re-orientated or reformed, it is our submission that hope will be rekindled for our Nation. If children and youth *"are taught to think for themselves, challenge questionable practices and be in control of their lives, there is hope for a better future"*.[49] This will surely yield the aims and objectives of the Nigerian Philosophy of Education which include:

1. *The inculcation of national consciousness and national unity.*

2. *The inculcation of the right type of values and attitudes for the survival of the individual and the Nigerian Society.*

3. *The training of the mind in the understanding of the world around.*

4. *The acquisition of appropriate skills, abilities and competences both mental and physical as equipment for the individual to live in and contribute to the development of his Society*[50]

---

[48] Felix K. Alonge et al., *Civic Education for Senior Secondary Schools 1*. Ibadan: University Press Plc, 2013, p. vi.

[49] Ezeanyino M. Nkechinyelu, "Citizenship and Civic Education", yet to be published in the Catholic Theological Association of Nigeria Proceedings, 2019, p. 5.

[50] Dr. Olusegun Akinbote, U.I. Ibadan, Origin and Development of Early Childhood Education. National Open University of Nigeria. Lagos: Express Image, 2006, pp. Unit 10, The National Policy on Education, 3.1.1.

The Socratic Method is equally appropriate or rather indispensable for moral instructions, besides the Civic Education. If this method is effectively applied in the areas mentioned above – Civic and Moral or Religious Education – there is no doubt about the recovery of the human values necessary for appropriate human life. Value here implies that intrinsic worth of a thing, that which is inherent in the nature of a thing. In other words, value of things does not depend on the whims and caprices of individuals, that is, on what I or any other person, for instance, takes to be valuable for me/him/her. Such values include: love of God and human beings, life, peace, justice, patriotism, integrity, honesty, truth, hard work, solidarity, et cetera. We believe that people discover and appropriate the values they live with through philosophical reflection which the Socratic Method is intended to facilitate. *"It is only critical, unbiased reflection that will enable people discover the values inherent in life and all it (life) presents, and so appropriate them either as a group in terms of cultural values, or as individuals in terms of personal values".*[51] We must note here that the transformation of cultural/societal values presupposes the transformation of personal or individual values. As the people are, so the society in which they live.

Besides, the grown-ups equally need civic education. We suggested somewhere else that *"our politicians should make civic education part of their retreat program for more effective delivery of their political mandates".*[52] It is not just for their political life but their all-round human life so as to be true models for the young ones. To say that many Nigerians are uncivilized is to say the least judging from their behavior, utterances, relationships, et cetera, hence the present state of our Nation. If anything, this Nation is in dire need of real good mentors in good manner of thinking, speaking and acting.

But someone may query – how long will this training take in order to produce the desired result? The method requires patience both on the part of the would-be teachers and the Society as well. Nobody should expect immediate result but whether the result should come is sure even if with generations to come. A popular saying has it that nothing good comes with ease. For anything worth the effort, one needs patience and endurance or perseverance, which are individual and cultural values as well.

---

[51] Rev. Sr. (Dr). Nkechi Ezeanyino, D.D.L., "Philosophy, Value and Human Development: A Panacea for Misplaced Priorities", op. cit. p. 140.

[52] Op. Cit., p. 9.

# Chapter 5

# The Cultural Relevance of Education

Sylvanus Ifeanyichukwu Nnoruka

**Abstract**

Every individual has the innate capacity of being educated. Authentic education incorporates the basic aspects of human formation: physical, mental, moral. While recognizing the relevance of the known theories of education and taking Africa and precisely the Igbo cultural group as our case study, with the illumination of the hermeneutical method, we argue and assert that for any educational system to correctly and positively influence the individual, it must be relevant to his/her environment; it must recognize the *who* of the individual. The individual thus educated is a balanced person who also recognizes the relevance of the other. It is only thus that education can contribute to the fulfillment and happiness of the individual, the peace and development of the environment and the entire humanity.

**Introduction**

Education from the etymological meaning has to do with the human person – process of leading out the potentialities latent in an individual. It means that every individual has the capacity of being educated. Education prepares the individual for real life with his social community as the starting point. Education no matter its cultural origin is a process; it is a training process. It trains the physical, mental and moral aspects of man and thereby prepares him for the duties of life. Authentic education incorporates the basic aspects of human formation: physical, mental, moral. Historically, it has had different dimensions among different peoples. Among the Spartans, education was administered by the State authority and was centered on the virtue of courage or 'spirited' element. In contrast to the Spartans, the Athenian Educational system was more private than public. The parents hired the services of private tutors for the training of their children. An educated Athenian could quote Homer and Hesiod. Plato was the first theorist of education. For him, education aims at good life and harmony in the State. The terrain was the Academy. For Aristotle, the primary purpose of education was qualification into the *polis*. It has moral undertone and emphasizes reason as well. It aims at achieving happiness. The terrain was the *Lyceum*. In the other epochs up till our time, education has been described from various perspectives – analytic, prescriptive, social science, normative, pragmatic, and denotative.

The achievements of these perspectives which portray themselves as standard-bearers notwithstanding, the position of our paper is that they have seriously imperiled the basic objective of education as preparation for real life in the community. We argue that every individual is a product of a culture, his first contact with the world is from a specific environment. His initial upbringing is inevitably influenced by this environment. For any educational system to influence this individual correctly and positively, it must be relevant to his environment. It must recognize the *who* of the individual.

## Historical Circumstances that Shaped the *Who* of the African of Today

One of the outstanding questions posed today with respect to Africa is: Why is Africa the way it is? What is wrong with Africa? Why is it that there is an unmistakable record of growth and development in every continent of the world except in Africa? Why is the African continent replete with tale of woes and disappointments? The answer to these questions should precede the formulation of any educational objective or method for Africa. Another way of asking the question is: What factors hitherto played significant roles in the shaping of the *who* of the African. We offer the following as a response: slave trade, colonialism, military regime, and neo-colonialism. These mark the various stages of the moral, psychological, physical degradation of the African.

We analyze slave trade in considerable detail. European attitudes to Africans in those early times before the slave trade had uniform characteristic; "they supposed no natural inferiority in Africans, no inherent failure to develop and maturity." Thus, in the early days of the discovery of Africa, Europe was convinced they had found partners and allies. In fact, they regarded Africans as equals. It was in this understanding that in 1563 Ramusio, secretary to the rulers of Venice, urged the merchants of Italy to go and do business with the king of Timbuktu and Mali. He had no doubt whatsoever that these merchants would be well received in Africa and consequently obtain the favors they ask.

Race contempt only crept in when those regarded as free men or slave dealers were able to fulfill their material interest and ambitions through the scorn and contempt they had for slaves. These slaves were men "to whom an unnatural inferiority had given every appearance of a natural inferiority." It is only so that intelligent men like Thomas Jefferson reached the conclusion that they did. He compared Africans in North America by their faculties of memory, reason and imagination. This was after more than a century of intensive slave trading had taken place. His conclusion was that in memory the blacks were equal to the whites but in reason much inferior. For him a black was incapable "of tracing and comprehending the investigations of Euclid; and that in imagination they are dull, tasteless and anomalous."[53]

To be treated as an inferior is often to become an inferior. The Americans and Europeans applied this principle so persistently and repeatedly that African history at the time was an analysis of the European state of mind as well as the African condition. Three hundred years into the trade, Europe was sure that "Africans had never so much as known the rudiments of political organizations, let alone the means of building powerful states and operating central governments: Africa it would be commonly said, simply lacked the faculty for growing up. Professor Keane writing in 1896 with a sort of assured Victorian complacency observed that their mental inferiority, which he insisted was inherent and more marked than their physical characters, depends on physiological causes. Earlier Richard Burton had maintained that once an African grew beyond childhood, 'his mental development is arrested, and thenceforth he grows backwards instead of forwards'."[54]

---

[53] Basil Davidson, *The African Slave Trade*, Little, Brown and Company, London, 1961, 25.

[54] Ibid., 26.

We maintain that slavery is devastating to the African man and continent. Our principal reason is that before the trade, the old states of Africa were organized and strong and "were seldom or never conquered from outside the continent." That is, they resisted invasion and remained inviolate. It would be too simplistic and naïve to explain away this fact of successful African resistance (as some tried to do) by reference to climate and mosquito. Clearer and objective "early records indicate another and more persuasive safeguard against conquest. They point to the striking power of African armies. They show that it was the military factor, time and again, which proved decisive."[55] A characteristic of old African states was unmistakable pride. Referring to northern Angola, Father Cavazziin 1687 complained that with nauseating presumption "these nations think themselves the foremost men in the world and nothing will persuade them to the contrary." For them, Africa is not only the greatest part of the world; it is also the happiest and most agreeable. The King himself held the same opinion in a more remarkable way. He was convinced that no other Monarch in the world was his equal and that he was the most powerful and richest of them all. So old Africa had flamboyant and unmistakable self-confidence. Davidson observes that the reasons were not obscure.

> They were the fruit of a long social development. The steady growth of Iron Age productive power and an improving command of environment; the evolution of new forms of self-government; the formaïon of kingships, the raising of armies, the swearing-in of vassals: all these and much else had signaled the processes of this development over many previous centuries. Increasingly, states had emerged. Now, often enough, they had become strong states whose central power rested on taut structures of lord-and-vassal dependence.[56]

---

[55] Ibid., 27.

[56] Ibid., 29.

Our task is now to propose an educational system which we are convinced will restore this self-confidence. It is a call for the restoration of the status quo.

## African Pragmatism

Etymologically, pragmatism has to do with pragma, from the Greek *prasso* – doing, acting. In Aristotle, it is the sphere of thought and action that comprises the ethical and political life of man as contrasted with theoretical designs of logic and epistemology, *theoria*. It is thus that praxis in a general sense means practice.

In philosophy, it stresses the relation of theory and praxis. Such a relationship takes the continuity of experience and nature as revealed through the outcome of directed action as the starting point of reflection. It means in effect that both subject and object are constituted in the process. What guides knowledge to become interests and values. It is also not possible to know the reality of objects prior to experience. So, truth claims can be justified only as a fulfillment of conditions that are experimentally determined; that is, the outcome of inquiry. Emphasis is on reciprocity of theory and praxis, knowledge and action, facts and values. Knowledge is understood as instrumental – a tool for organizing experience satisfactorily. Concepts become habits of belief or rules of action. Epistemological criteria are no longer the sole determinant of truth. This is because the adequacy of these criteria cannot be determined apart from the goals sought and values instantiated. These assertions also have implications for culture. It concerns the ways values which arise in historically specific cultural situations can be appropriated. They can be intelligently appropriated only to the extent that they satisfactorily resolve problems and are judged worth retaining.

It follows that pragmatism as a philosophical movement can be relevant to Africa. Using it as a starting point, one can construct an African pragmatic theory of education. Such a theory is not a reproduction of philosophical pragmatism; it has only some of the traits of philosophical pragmatism. A distinguishing characteristic of the theory is that it is rooted in African culture. Pragmatism is only a philosophical light that we are using to illuminate it. It is utility oriented but not in the sense of pure economic value. It is rather development oriented, precisely human development. Every other value derives from this development orientation. The root could be traced from old African states. It derives from them and has its relevance only with reference to them.

The old African states had a clear and unmistakable purpose of education – functionalism. This was the principal guiding principle. It was a means to an end. It formed part of the immediate induction into the society. The content prepares the young for adulthood. It is maturity-oriented and embraces theory and practice. It is aimed at molding a balanced personality for the society. Social responsibility, job orientation, political participation, spiritual and moral values were the cardinal aspects of it. The principle of *Faber fabricando fit* was applied. The young learnt by doing. It was a sort of participatory education. This was conducted through ceremonies, rituals, imitation, recitation and demonstration. Pragmatic education had many dimensions such as practical farming, fishing, weaving, cooking, carving, and knitting, to name but a few. Recreational dimension or subjects include wrestling, dancing, drumming, acrobatic display, and racing. There was in old Africa intellectual training which was made up of the following subjects: local history, legends, the environment (geography, zoology, botany) poetry, reasoning riddles, proverbs, story-telling, story-relays, etc. A unique characteristic of education in this sense is that it is an integrated experience. This means that it is not purely intellectual, rather combined physical training with character-building, manual activity with intellectual training. Each stage is demarcated either by age level or years of exposure. At the end there was examination in form of practical test relevant to the candidate's years of exposure. Continuous assessment was also part of the examination. The final stage is the 'passing out' ceremony. Characteristically, this ceremony is initiation into adulthood.

The next stage is for the select of the elect. They go through the secret cults. The cults served as institutions of power (the debate on whether they are real or imaginary is not our concern here). At this stage, "profound native philosophy, science and religion were mastered".[57]

---

[57] A. Babs Fafunwa, *History of Education in Nigeria*, George Allen & Unwin, London, 1974, 16.

Every level of education in old Africa had functional character and, in our formulation, pragmatic. We maintain this position because curriculum was relevant to the needs of life. Unemployment in many African states today is regrettably at exceedingly high percentage. In old African society, if it existed at all, it was minimal. Today, many trained unemployed men and women roam the villages and towns. In old African society, it was minimal to the extent of being negligible.

We can now summarize the basic characteristics of education in traditional African society to include collective and social in nature. The latter means that it has intimate ties with social life in both the material and spiritual sense. It is multivalent. The achievements are gradual and progressive. They also conform to the various stages of physical, emotional and mental development of the child. It is clear that indigenous education does not completely conform to the ways of the western system. It is on account of this factor that some not-so well-informed writers have tagged it primitive. Some refer to it even as savage or barbaric. Fafunwa sees such contentions "as the product of ignorance and due to a total misunderstanding of the inherent value of an educational system." The determinant factor in evaluating any educational system is the extent to which it is meeting the needs of a society at any given time. "Traditional African education must therefore be judged not by any extraneous consideration or some foreign yardstick but by its performance within a given social context."[58]

We deem it necessary at this stage to make our point clearer through a detailed examination of a subject in African traditional education – African drama. In most cases, there is the use of narrative in performance. Here, most societies in Africa have story-telling tradition. The Igbo of southern Nigeria have the story of the tortoise, the Akan in Ghana the stories of *Ananse* the tricky spider. The Ijaw cultural community of Southern Nigeria has an epic narrative tradition. For the complete saga to be told, it requires many evenings. "Very often the story-teller is a lone performer (with, perhaps, some accompaniment by musicians) and his art lies in his ability to get his audience to participate in the telling of the story without the story-teller himself losing the 'ownership' of it."[59] The Kwagh hir puppet

---

[58] Ibid., 17.

[59] Michael Etherton, *The Development of African Drama*, African Publishing Company, New York, 1982, 39.

theatre among the Tiv is a story-telling theatre. Even though it appears today in a highly complex and active form, it is purely a rural traditional art. It was earlier linked to the cult riots of the colonial period and latter to the Tiv riots of 1960. Today, it is a modern theatrical art of performance; but its rural and wholly indigenous root should never be de-emphasized. There is a combination of spectacle and performance. The spectacle derives from the plastic arts – the masks and figurines of monsters and humans. Songs, dances and stories constitute the performance milieu. "The stories and their presentation as spectacle are a metaphor for the Tiv world view. This involves the traditional beliefs in magic, and in acquisition, by individuals, of 'powers' and influence, being secularized and commented upon in public: the dolls and masks, which were part of the cult world, are brought out into the public gaze in a stylized but essentially non-affective way."[60]

We should also make reference to the annual *Kalankuwa* festival in Borno. It started as a harvest festival. It "is dominated by the role-play performances of the young adults of the village who are the organizers."[61] Many of the villagers do not go to sleep that night. Some university-trained theatre artists who witnessed it on invitation saw that it bore no relation to their concept of drama. Their principal difficulty came with the role-play which they observed to be "so serious and so meticulously observed" that they had "some difficulty knowing who was in role and who was actually a member of the village hierarchy." They also found it difficult to know who was in role and who was not.[62] The performance that these university lecturers and students witnessed surely did not correspond to their conception of drama. They saw drama different from the farmers' point of view. Some even felt that the village farmers appropriated the word 'drama' to describe their own cultural presentation. Some of them were even of the view that the village farmers "need to be organized." Here is a manifestation of two different views of the word 'organization'; the village farmers' conception of organization and that as conceived by professional theatre and drama unit of the university. To be noted is that organization by village farmers was at the grassroots and at the very

---

[60] Ibid., 40.

[61] Ibid., 29.

[62] Ibid., 30.

lowest social and cultural level. A member of the university group gave credence to this by attesting that the villagers were organized:

> …the ability of these young adults to form such a grass-roots organization that mobilized *cadres* to raise money, collect costumes, improvise imaginatively on decoration, borrow expensive equipment, and then ensure that the two-day festival ran smoothly, probably exceeded the organizational capability, at a comparable level, of the professional theatre and drama units in the university who have more resources at their disposal. It certainly exceeded these units' ability to present performances in rural villages.[63]

The farmers further manifested their organizational ability by integrating presentation of prizes within the context of performance itself. It is only when one understands *Kalankuwa* as a harvest festival that this integration becomes meaningful.

Unfortunately, the Borno *Kalankuwa* is not an adequate representation of the way drama should develop from the traditional culture. This is because the "present-day *Kalankuwa* performance in Borno village might seem to be trivial, inconsequential, and even a corruption of tradition for it is changing from a harvest festival into a more satirical festival with license to 'break the rules' for the duration."[64] What ought to be the case is the transformation of the festival by modern drama while maintaining its roots and the original meaning as harvest festival. Modern drama should use its tools to shed light on the festival. It is only the maintenance of the original meaning that guarantees its authenticity. To develop in any other way is an abuse. Heidegger's notion of the development of arts as expressed in his *The Origin of the Work of Arts* can be of immense help here.

## Indispensable Contents of African Pragmatism

We deem the following to be indispensable aspects of the educational

---

[63] Ibid., 31.

[64] Ibid., 34.

program: development, poverty alleviation, conflict resolution, intercultural studies, forgiveness, phenomenology and hermeneutics.

The first is development program. The problem of Africa is basically that of human development; by this we mean integral human development. Africans are faced with widespread poverty, ill health, and lack of educational opportunities. Despite the positive political developments of the late 20th century, many African governments have been unable to improve their peoples' standards of living. The foundation of Africa's disadvantaged position has been its economic role in the world trading system.

Poverty as a social problem is a deeply embedded wound that permeates every dimension of culture and society. It includes sustained low levels of income for members of a community. There is also lack of access to services like education, markets, health care, lack of decision-making ability, and lack of communal facilities like water, sanitation, roads, transportation, and communications. Furthermore, it is a "poverty of spirit," that allows members of that community to believe in and share despair, hopelessness, apathy, and timidity. Poverty, especially the factors that contribute to it, is a social problem, and its solution is social. Despite all the wealthy resources in its possession, Africa is the world's poorest continent. We enumerate some of the outstanding causes of poverty in Africa: poor land utilization, civil wars and unending political conflicts, poor infrastructure, the World Bank and IMF policies, global distribution of resources, poor governance which in most cases lead to conflict, corruption, environmental degradation, disease, and lack of proper concept of freedom.

There is also conflict resolution. It concerns principally evolving a way or ways of overcoming the following: prejudice, interpreting the world only from the perspective of one's cultural group. We can call it "cultural self-imprisonment", racial discrimination. The basic question to be addressed here is: "Why do conflicts persist in Africa?" Our prompt response is that it persists because no proper educational program has been formulated to address the issue.

There are also intercultural studies. These are necessary because the world and Africa in particular is a multi-cultural community. Africa has at least fifty-five countries. The countries are made up of about one thousand ethnic groups, each with its own specific culture and language.

There are similarities and wide range of differences among these cultures. It follows that one cannot from a study of a particular culture in Africa make generalizations with regard to other cultures. Intercultural studies simply mean dialogue with other cultures; conversation with other cultures, disposition to appreciate another culture the way it manifests itself.

Forgiveness should also form a key part of our educational curriculum. This has become necessary on account of the many conflicts and crimes against humanity that have taken place in Africa. Some of them are apartheid and genocide. Forgiveness here does not mean that the forgiving party no longer accepts that it was brutally injured and psychologically deformed. Nor does it mean that the injuries and deformations have been forgotten. It simply means in spite of the regrettable past, let us establish a point of contact, let us reestablish dialogue. It is only in this way that past injuries would gradually heal and a better and peaceful future would be possible.

Phenomenology and hermeneutics are philosophical methods that were developed to maturity within the twentieth century. Edmund Husserl and Heidegger could be cited as outstanding in the former while for the latter we cite Gadamer and Paul Ricoeur. Both enable us to analyze reality especially cultural values without bias or presupposition. Reality should first and foremost be allowed to manifest itself as it is. We do not necessarily depend on any method to arrive at the truth.

## Conclusion

The position of this paper ought to be so far unequivocally clear: Education is for the good of the individual and the progress of the society; by this we mean the environment where the particular individual finds himself; the environment that marks his contact with the world, Heidegger's *umwelt*. It means the integral development of the individual with his initial environment as the starting point. We mean here not just the Cartesian knowing man (cogito). We rather mean here a type of education whose program takes into consideration Kant's three basic questions: what can I know? what can I do? what can I hope for? Every aspect of man here comes into consideration: social, cultural, ethical, moral, and political. It is only from a being so educated that adequate action follows – *agere sequitor esse*. The product of such an educational system is not just an individual who is simply a laborer in the society or an individual who is simply a worker in the society like a teacher, office clerk, policeman, bank worker etc. The product is rather an individual who performs adequate action within the society. Our illumination here is from Hannah Arendt's distinction. She distinguishes between thinking and working. A thinker who wants the world to share his thoughts must stop thinking and remember his thoughts. Remembering becomes the beginning of the work process. On the other hand, labor does not reveal the *who* of the individual because it is destructive and devouring, it is "relentless repetition" and lacks courage. Work changes matter, works upon it, and uses it as finished product. Work guarantees the durability of the world. A more interesting distinction for us is that made between work and action. Action is higher than work because it discloses the agent, the *who*.[65] So the type of education we are proposing is not simply for a meal ticket. It is integral training of the human person, who thereafter becomes able to distinguish good from bad; who is unequivocally convinced that bribery and corruption destroys both the individual and the society; that development is much more than construction of good roads and making political propaganda with the provision of basic amenities. Rather it is the human person who recognizes that education is not static but a continuous process, one who is ever disposed for the leading out of his latent potentialities through reading, belief in the transcendent Being; critically open both to those in his environment and to people of other cultures. It is only so that education can contribute to the fulfillment and happiness of the individual, the peace and development of the environment and the entire humanity.

---

[65] Hannah Arendt, *The Human Condition*, The University of Chicago Press, 1958, pp. 175-180.

# Chapter 6

# The Law of Emergent Probability and National Development

Humphrey Uchenna Ani.

## Introduction

Laws and regulations have been made and enacted in the search for solutions to national problems in Nigeria. But most times, these laws and constitutions have not yielded much positive results because the personalities of the individuals who should execute them have not been formed for efficient applications. The problem with Nigeria is not about laws and rules, but about people who should have the duty and good will to put them into practice. Best laws make no meaning when not applied. And the best national visions will have no effect and impact if they are not expressed in action and practical development. Therefore, this presentation intends to look at the problem of Nigeria as coming from the wrong development of the Nigerian personality before looking at the social impacts of such wrong development in the national development project. It is a kind of down-to-top approach to the Nigerian national development project, using what Bernard Lonergan called the law of emergent probability. This submission will look at the idea of the law of emergent probability, from its background and scope, and develop ways its related method and principles can be used to evaluate and approach the development plans in Nigeria.

## The Law of Emergent Probability

To understand the law of emergent probability in Lonergan, one would need to understand the intellectual grid from which he crafted this law. The law of emergent probability actually was propounded within the context of definition of method of understanding by Lonergan.[66] Method of understanding was formulated to guide the development of human consciousness which plays out in various aspects of human development in general. We shall discuss this in detail after we have explained what the law of emergent probability means.

The law of emergent probability according to Lonergan says that there is an order in the universe often captured in the classical and statistical laws, in which there are internal structures of schemes of recurrent activities which yield new results when the conditions of the earlier schemes are fulfilled and functioning well. The law of emergent probability derives from the operations of both classical and statistical intelligibility. Classical intelligibility involves systematic and controlled conditions that must be met before a certain law is held to be true or a given result is held like in the law of gravity or germination. Statistical intelligibility on the contrary goes with non-systematic aggregate of events and sequence before a result is achieved like in human moral law.[67] While the classical intelligibility is often based on the constant nature of things, the statistical intelligibility is often based on the unpredictable schemes like the exercise of human freedom.

A typical example of classical intelligibility can be seen in the procedure of germination and growth of plants. A plant has to sprout or germinate before it can grow. It has to grow before it can develop stems. The stems have to mature before it can have leaves and flowers. And these have to be in place before the plant can produce fruit. This law of emergent probability holds that the condition for growth and subsequent emergence of stems, leaves, flowers and fruits, depend on the satisfaction of germination and subsequent order of growth and production of fruit. It would be awkward to find a plant producing fruits without germination and growth. These earlier conditions that make production of fruits possible is what Lonergan refers to as "recurrent schemes", which are the elements or simplest forms of dynamic activities that recur and generate subsequent actions unto fruition.

---

[66] Lonergan called his idea of method a "Generalized Empirical Method (GEM)".

[67] Cf. Bernard Lonergan, Insight: *A Study of Human Understanding*, ed. F.E. Crowe and R. Doran, CWL, III (Toronto: University of Toronto Press, 1992), 43-44.

The law of emergent probability means that the condition for the probable emergence of new effects depends on the conditions of earlier operations. A functioning scheme fulfills the condition for the probability of emergence and survival of the later schemes. It argues that "combinations of events possess a probability, and that probability jumps, first when a scheme becomes concretely possible in virtue of the fulfillment of its prior conditions, and secondly when the scheme begins actually to function."[68] This law however does not claim that one scheme directly causes another. This would be deterministic. It rather suggests that the probable emergence of a subsequent scheme depends on the existence of the preceding one.[69] "The actual functioning of earlier schemes in the series fulfils the conditions of the probability of the functioning of later schemes."[70] This implies that in the operations of the human mind and development, a certain principle is followed. This principle holds that attention has to be paid to things as the condition for the probability of understanding about them to emerge. Understanding will become the fulfillment of the condition for critical handling of issues, which also fulfills the condition for the emergence of right decision over them. It is made to guide the method of understanding and general development of individuals and groups according to Lonergan. He gave this law to guide the method of development of human consciousness and the human community subsequently.

## Developmental Method and Law of Emergent Probability

Method in general for Lonergan refers to "a normative pattern of recurrent and related operations yielding cumulative and progressive results."[71] He further explained that in method, there are distinct operations, where each operation is related to the others, and the set of relations form a pattern. This pattern is described as the right way of

---

[68] Ibid.144-150.

[69] Cf. Gerard Whelan, *Redeeming History-Social Concern in Bernard Lonergan and Robert Doran* (Rome: Gregorian and Biblical Press, 2013), 77.

[70] Lonergan, Insight: A Study of Human Understanding, 145.

[71] Bernard Lonergan, *Method in Theology* (Toronto: University of Toronto Press, 1972), 4.

doing a job, and its operations in accord with the pattern may be repeated indefinitely, leading to cumulative and progressive results.[72] Method of understanding and development is a dynamic process which is normative, recurrent, cumulative, and progressive, involving the heightening of the mind and operations to any intelligible object and reality. That is to say that human knowledge and action are the results of method.[73] Lonergan argues that any method that can succeed follows four transcendental precepts or principles, and these principles are governed by the law of emergent probability if they have to achieve their desired objectives. The four transcendental principles or methodic steps of consciousness and development include:

## The Empirical Level

At this precept, method demands that one pays attention to empirical things around oneself. The mind at this level is formed to recognize the empirical world around it. Conscious attention to the physical environment implies making the mind aware of physical realities, needs, desires and values, which it has to deal with. Minds are to be shaped to be conscious of the "how" of existence. How do I get my particular needs fairly resolved? How do I keep to a healthy living—healthy nutrition, healthy psyche, healthy relationships and healthy environment? How do I save to protect myself from the lack of basic needs? How do I relate with others? How do I manage intrapersonal, interpersonal, family and community conflicts? How is one's mind heightened to such realities like the physical presence of others, physical aesthetics and physical decency which Lonergan represented as "particular good."[74] The mind is trained through education at this rudimentary level to be aware and to form a genuine strategy to procure and manage basic empirical needs like food, shelter, clothing, relationship, human characters and human labour. It is also trained to satisfy them by just, fair and decent means and to appreciate how they mediate the higher structures of one's existentiality.

---

[72] Cf. Lonergan, Method in Theology, 4.

[73] Cf. Michael Shute, *The Origins of Lonergan's Notion of the Dialectic of History* (Lanham: University Press of America, Inc, 1951), 14.

[74] Cf. J. Ogbonnaya, Lonergan, *Social Transformation, and Sustainable Human Development* (Oregon: Wipf and Stock Publishers, 2013), 94.

The empirical precept of consciousness in man can be seen in seven patterns of sensitive experiences: biological, aesthetic, dramatic, practical, social, intellectual and mystical.[75] Forming and raising one's consciousness to immediate physical experiences can help one engage in the cultivation of one's physical empowerment, achieving physical satisfaction, building basic human skills, know-how, physical good and learning to provide basic needs and to realize personal contentment, self-worth and personal peace. At this level, one needs to make the mind have what John Dewey calls "active intelligence",[76] through which one can apply one's thinking into action in order to procure physical good for rudimentary survival and sound personality. It is such a sound mind and satisfied personality that lays the first foundation necessary for personal and national development.

## The Intellectual Level

If one is sound and satisfied, one will be disposed to engage in intellectual activities which form the second level of consciousness development. At the intellectual level of methodic development, normative patterns of operations are put in place to intelligently comprehend or organize the world around oneself. This involves forming the mind to engage in deeper understanding and pursuance of answers to questions of Why? or What for? of the things around oneself. This implies making inquiries, generating insight and formulations of systems that help in organizing oneself and one's society. Here, accumulated insights are expressed in intelligent application, grasp of situations and mastery of theoretical and practical domains.[77] This level creates what Lonergan calls "the 'good of the order' to ensure the recurrence of schemes of events or structures for the provision of the 'physical good' not only for oneself but for other people who are members of the civil community."[78] The good of the order "consists in an intelligible pattern of relationships that

[75] Cf. B. Lonergan, Insight: A Study of Human Understanding, 205-231.

[76] Cf. S. E. Stumpf & *J. Fieser, Philosophy: History and Problems* (New York: Lisa Moore, 2008), 381.

[77] Cf. B. Lonergan, Method in Theology, 10.

[78] J. Ogbonnaya, Lonergan, Social Transformation, and Sustainable Human Development, 94.

conditions the fulfillment of each man's desire by his contributions to the fulfillment of the desires of others, and similarly protects each from the object of his fears in the measure he contributes to warding off the objects feared by others."[79] Good of the order implies intellectual "products of practical intelligence as the polity, the economic, technology, social arrangements like marriage and family as an institution."[80]

If people are intellectually well formed, they will be able to engage in corporation and specialization as a group, where all contribute to the society and receive benefits from the society in a mutual complementary manner.[81] They will be able to craft intelligent laws, create functional technology, strong economy, peaceful polity and good family structures that enhance national development. Having an intelligent citizenry and government who can organize a society into civil, critical, creative and transformative order is a major step in building a developed society. Intelligent citizens are more likely to imbibe civic discipline and to embrace patriotic demands which constitute the bedrock for national development and order. Of course, democratic principles can only function where there is thriving civic culture.[82] When citizens are properly guided by a clear national philosophy, they can build on that to embrace other principles such as fairness, secularity, equity, justice and impartiality in the national life.

**The Rational Level**

The third level of formation of the human mind for national development, would need to focus on critical development of the consciousness and attitude of the people. But this must be preceded by the establishment of a civil society with intelligent citizenry. Here understanding, stereotypes, beliefs, traditions, customs and structures

---

[79] B. Lonergan, Insight: A Study of Human Understanding, 238.

[80] Cf. J. Ogbonnaya, Lonergan, Social Transformation, and Sustainable Human Development, 94.

[81] Brian Cronin, *Value Ethics: A Lonergan Perspective* (Nairobi: Consolata Institute of Philosophy Press, 2006), 146.

[82] In many political societies power can be exercised through four main operative systems: dictatorship, traditional authority, persuasion/manipulation and democracy.

of existentiality are evaluated. A critical citizenry can lead to widespread personal culture of objectivity among citizens, deep sense of valid judgments and unbiased assessment and evaluation of personal and social issues. "There is the potential for the general analysis of interiority grounded in self-appropriation which could count for the whole realm of proportionate being."[83] People at this level are supposed to evolve a more authentic anthropological personality that is guided by rational or moral decisions. The goal would be to create the "good as the possible object of rational choice,"[84] whereby the human subject makes rational and responsible choices, modifying the society as virtuous persons capable of building a solid and healthy civilization with others.[85] This implies the transformation of cultural values, constituting a yardstick for measuring, judging and evaluating the physical and social goods that bind the nation together. This creative period is where the higher powers of reason and judgment can provide the superstructures that govern the infrastructural achievements of the practical and technological faculties of citizens in the society. If Nigeria should get to this level of development of consciousness, it would be easier for Nigerians to be more law abiding, patriotic, detribalized, fair, just and impartial in handling national issues. And this will be a big plus in the national development project, especially in building strong human resources.

## The Responsible Level

At this level of mind formation, one learns to make responsible decisions. One is habituated to face definite demands in life: "to do or not to do". There are some questions that arise at this level: what is it to be done with what one has known and judged right? Will one's decision over the insight be beneficial or not, and could it be right when made? It is a moral cross-road at one's journey in formation, where one may decide to follow the provisions of insight or decide against it. If at this level of consciousness, one makes a decision based on the truth of insight and judgment, one's action could emerge to be right and good,

---

[83] Shute, The Origins of Lonergan's Notion of the Dialectic of History, 44-45.

[84] B. Lonergan, Insight: A Study of Human Understanding, 624.

[85] B. Lonergan, Method in Theology, 34.

and one will be considered authentic. But if one decides on the contrary, one's action could be wrong and bad, and it will be considered inauthentic and bad. Authenticity is the bedrock for national development. Authenticity means being attentive to the experiences around oneself; exercising intelligent understanding over one's experiences; critically making reasonable judgments over what one understands and taking responsible decision based on one's reasonable judgment. It is the achievement of self-transcendence through the transcendental precepts: being attentive, intelligent, reasonable and responsible.[86] This implies cultivating the beauty of goodness, peace culture, good of value, higher values, dignity, respect, truth, social consciousness, accountable governance, civilized citizenry, development of decent attitudes and responsible morality and religiosity.

## Conclusion

In the application of the law of emergent probability to national development therefore, one must start from the formation of characters of individual citizens that make up the nation. One cannot talk of national development if the individuals are undeveloped. The condition for national development to thrive must be satisfied in the full development of the individuals, otherwise, such will be like putting the cart before the horse. The second dimension of the application is that in the development of the individual and the nation, there must be an intelligent method which follows the transcendental precepts. That method demands that development must start from the basics, to progress to the higher levels. It means that there must be proper formation of citizens who pay attention to basic empirical or physical factors and needs around them. Being able to do this will prepare the ground for them to be able to engage in more intellectual participations. A hungry society cannot produce thinking citizens. And unintelligent citizens are less likely to be critical, objective and sincere in moral and even religious issues. The condition for the probable emergence of a critical and objective society is to have an intelligent system and society. And the condition for the possible emergence of honest, ethical and authentic religious people in a society is to have a society where people are objective and sincere in their judgments.

---

[86] Cf. B. Lonergan, Method in Theology, 9.

The submission of this paper therefore is that the task of national development in Nigeria must start in the formation and development of the individual Nigerians. The emergence of developed Nigeria is only possible in the development of individual Nigerians, not just a making bogus state and national policies. This formation must equally start from the rudiments to the firmaments. It must start by paying attention to the basic elements for material growth and development. It must satisfy this before it can build an intelligent social structure that functions and which will be sustainable. This is what will provide the necessary conditions for the emergence of a civil society in which Nigerians can cultivate and live with a culture of higher values and authenticity in both moral and spiritual matters. This has to be the condition for national development order. The contrary will be efforts in futility.

## Bibliography


Cronin, Brian. *Value Ethics: A Lonergan Perspective*, Nairobi: Consolata Institute of Philosophy Press, 2006.

Lonergan, Bernard. *Insight: A Study of Human Understanding.* Edited by F.E. Crowe and R. Doran. CWL. 3. Toronto: University of Toronto Press, 1992.

*Method in Theology.* Toronto: University of Toronto Press, 1972.

Ogbonnaya, Joseph. *Lonergan, Social Transformation, and Sustainable Human Development.* Oregon: Wipf and Stock Publishers, 2013.

Shute, Michael. *The Origins of Lonergan's Notion of the Dialectic of History.* Lanham: University Press of America, Inc, 1951.

Stumpf, Samuel and Fieser, James. *Philosophy, History and Problems.* New York: Lisa Moore, 2008.

Whelan, George. *Redeeming History-Social Concern in Bernard Lonergan and Robert Doran.* Rome: Gregorian and Biblical Press, 2013.

# Chapter 7

# The Modern Sophists in Religious Garb: The Nigerian Experience

Modestus Anyaegbu

## Introduction

The choice of the topic "the Modern Sophists in Religious Garb" is quite *ad rem* and traditional. Those we refer to as 'Modern Sophists' in this write up are the religious leaders of Pentecostal Churches. Whether they refer to themselves as 'Bishops, Evangelists, or Prophets', the one term that englobes them is 'Pastor' and we wish to represent all those religious men and women in the Pentecostal industry in Nigeria as 'Pentecostal Pastors.' Lately, a small number of catholic priests by their activities, have also become 'modern sophists in religious garb.' In the ancient Athens, sophistry took on a negative and dangerous meaning that it became harmful for people to publicly identify themselves as Sophists. To continue practicing their art, they had to disguise themselves and work under cover. According to Plato in one of his dialogues, "Some used poetry as a screen, for instance Homer and Hesiod and Simonides; others religious rites and prophecy, like Orpheus and Musaeus and their school; some even—so I have noticed—physical training, like Iccus of Tarentum…all of them, as I say, used these arts as a screen to escape malice."[87] If the practice were true of the ancient Athenians, we could say the same today though not for the same purpose. We refer to the Pentecostal Pastors in the

---

[87] Plato, Protagoras 316d-317a, All quotations from the dialogues are taken from *The Collected Dialogues of Plato*, edited by Hamiltion and Huntington Cairns, (New Jersey: Princeton University Press, 1989).

Nigerian Pentecostal Industry as modern Sophists because their art is the same as the ancient Sophists—rhetorics though in religious garb and practiced in religious environments. Prophets and those who practiced religious rites of various degrees were all Sophists but changed their names for protection against malice. Sophists in the ancient times attracted odium to themselves because of their art of sophistry.[88] Today the religious industry has become the umbrella for all modern Sophists—evangelists, pastors, healers, seers, miracle workers, prophets etc. Our study will establish why we think that what they do today in the so called "name of God" is nothing short of sophistry as they continue to parade themselves as 'unprincipled rogues,' attracting more unsuspecting folks. Protagoras the Sophist has a word of advice for his fellow Sophists. "I admit to being a Sophist and an educator, and I consider this a better precaution than the other—admission rather than denial."[89] It will be an insurmountable task demanding the modern-day sophists to assume their real identity just like Protagoras did. We shall attempt in this write up to justify that appellation by examining the concrete evidence of the methods and practices of Pentecostal Pastors in the booming Nigerian Industry of Pentecostalism. Just like in Athens, we shall draw the sophist-like effects of the practices of Pentecostalism in the lives of the Pentecostal followers and unsuspecting worshippers.

**1. The Sophists of the Fifth Century Athens:**
The Athens of old knew some intellectual and social or cultural progress in the fifth and fourth centuries. At that time, there was this need for a structural form of education beyond the ordinary training in military tactics and traditional ways of life. Democracy brought with it many challenges. Only those who could convince people about the questions of justice and the like had prospects of making it into political positions of authority. Thus, there was need for good public speakers and masterful speech-makers with the power to make even weaker arguments look the stronger.[90] Because of this need which Athens could not satisfy by itself, it welcomed teachers who claimed

---

[88] Ibid. 316d.

[89] Ibid. 317b.

[90] Plato, Apology 18b.

to be experts or professionals in teaching *areté*—virtue or excellence. These teachers came from neighbouring towns and cities into Athens to trade their professional wares and instructions in various subjects for money.[91] What we do not know precisely is whether they would have been willing to instruct the young without demanding money? Or Whether they were not actually motivated to offer their so-called expertise because of the monetary gain involved? The dialogues of Plato are replete with the emergence of these itinerant teachers claiming to be experts in a variety of subjects like politics and persuasive speaking. Would-be leaders found new opportunities to become better communicators and better leaders of army and nations—and hence, the success of the new teachers. As recorded by Plato, Protagoras claimed to teach any person entrusted to his care "the proper care of his personal affairs, so that he may best manage his own household, and also of the state's affairs, so as to become a real power in the city, both as speaker and man of action." In short, he would make men good citizens.[92] Gorgias claimed to be an expert in the art of rhetoric, that is, "the power to convince by your words the judges in court, the senators in council, the people in the Assembly, or in any other gathering of a citizen body."[93] Euthydemus with his brother Dionysodorus, (both Sophists though not as well known as the others) were reported to be men of wisdom who knew everything about war like Generals would, all about tactics and how to lead an army; moreover, they could make a man able to defend himself in the law courts. Over and above these, they specialized in teaching virtue: "We believe we can impart it—no one in the world so well or so quickly."[94] Hippias of Elis who spent his life representing governments as an ambassador, also prided himself in his possession of wisdom and in his ability to advance his pupils and associates in virtue.[95] Prodicus of Ceos was also a successful member of these itinerant teachers in the

---

[91] Anthony Kenny, *A New History of Western Philosophy*, (Oxford: Clarendon Press, 2010) p. 29.

[92] Plato, Protagoras 318e-319a.

[93] Plato, Gorgias 449a, 452e.

[94] Plato, Euthydemus 273c-d.

[95] Plato, Greater Hippias 281b, 283c.

Athens of around 5th century BC. Socrates testifies that "he was much admired for his eloquence before the Council, and also as a private person he made an astonishing amount of money by giving demonstrations to the young and admitting them to his society."[96] Though not explicitly mentioned in the dialogues, other sources indicate that Prodicus used his public lectures to inculcate virtue in his listeners. This group of itinerant teachers are generally called Sophists. They made Athens believe that success in life hinged on excellent and creative communication. As captured by Broadie:

> The sophists' staple, then, was the study and teaching of communication-skills for exercise in various fairly well defined civic situations. But they also stand for something larger and more nebulous, and their originality far outran innovations immediately relevant to producing good speakers for existing contexts.[97]

Sophist is from the Greek word *sophistes* meaning 'sage' or 'wise man' or 'master of a craft.'[98] However, with the incessant attacks by mostly Plato and Aristotle, the word came to take a predominantly negative connotation of 'clever' or 'sophistry.' The lack of documented evidence of their writings and speeches makes it difficult to ascertain from them who they actually thought they were and the objective or goal of their itinerary teachings. This lack makes it incontestable to rely on the abundance of written documentation on the Sophists and their art left by Plato and by Aristotle. As articulated by Kerferd in one of his numerous researches on the identity and mission of the Sophists:

> Not one barrier but two stand in the way of anyone who seeks to arrive at a proper understanding of the

---

[96] Ibid. 282c-d.

[97] Sarah Broadie, "The Sophists and Socrates" in *The Cambridge Companion to Greek and Roman Philosophy* (Cambridge: Cambridge University Press, 2003), pp. 74-75.

[98] Thomas A. Blackson, *Ancient Greek Philosophy: From the Presocratics to the Hellenistic Philosophers*, (West-Sussex: Wiley-Blackwell, 2011), p. 71.

sophistic movement at Athens in the fifth century BC.
No writings survive from any of the sophists and we
have to depend on the inconsiderable fragments and
often obscure or unreliable summaries of their
doctrines. What is worse, for much of our information
we are dependent upon Plato's profoundly hostile
treatment of them, presented with all the power of his
literary genius and driven home with a philosophical
impact that is little short of overwhelming.[99]

Kerferd's observation makes it look as if Plato set out to become inimical
to the Sophists. The truth is that Plato objectively X-rayed the Sophists,
their numerous methods and their messages and wanted actually to
distance Socrates from the unpalatable accusation that he too was also a
Sophist. This he did by putting to the full glare of everyone who cared
to see, the different methodologies and objectives of both Sophists and
Socrates. The abundance of literature on the identity of the Sophists
and their numerous methods in the various dialogues of Plato, show the
unbiased nature of his presentation of these itinerant teachers who
flocked into Athens and took advantage of the moment. It is thanks
largely to Plato that the inventions of the Sophists, their intellectual
contributions, their versatility in almost all fields of life, their excellent
public speeches one of which is seen in the passage of *Protagoras* 323c-
328c, their education of the Athenian youths and their incontestable
contributions to the development of the Athenian democracy have come
to be appreciated. If Plato was actually biased against these itinerant
teachers, he would have had no business highlighting their positives for
the world to see and appreciate. As a philosopher of the preeminent class,
Plato also had the sacred duty of engaging in argumentations with them
in order to see the solidity or not of their teachings. Fortunately, Plato's
arguments and critiques outclassed the best of what the Sophists had to
offer. It is from his numerous encounters with the Sophists and his
verification of their claims that Plato gives us his consistent view of the
Sophists in his numerous dialogues. Guthrie confirms that the negative
image the Sophists had was not initiated by Plato. According to him,

---

[99] G. B. Kerferd, *The Sophistic Movement*, (Cambridge: Cambridge University Press, 1981) p. 1.

"apart from the evidence of Xenophon, it would have been quite impossible for Plato to have referred, in the manner and the contexts in which he does so refer, to the paid teachers as Sophists if that had not been their recognized title."[100]

The Sophists according to Plato are those "who profess to be teachers of virtue and offer their services freely to any Greek who wishes to learn, charging a fixed fee for their instruction."[101] In a dialogue that bears the name of the *Sophists*, Plato describes the 'Sophist' as 'a sort of wizard, an imitator of real things—who does not possess genuine knowledge of all the things he seems capable of disputing about.'[102] In the language that assimilates the Sophists to the poets, Plato further describes them as image makers and creators of illusions. In what would contest for the harshest language used in the dialogues, Plato calls them 'hired hunters of rich young men because of the fees they will get, as merchants, as retail dealers, as manufacturers and salesmen of information.'[103] These various descriptions of the Sophists would again feature in details when we look at the criticisms levelled against them. Outside of the Platonic dialogues, the same meaning of money makers follow the word 'sophists.' Xenophon in his *Memorabilia* notes that "those who sell their wisdom for money to anyone who wants it are called Sophists."[104] Aristotle defines the Sophist as "one who makes money from an apparent but unreal wisdom."[105]

As is evident, the *areté*—excellence or virtue that these Sophists purported to teach was not primarily of ethical type, but a set of competences or abilities or skills needed for success in public life. It is not as if they all agreed to teach various competences. They were individuals who embarked upon a journey of trying to make money on the claim of teaching virtue. According to Taylor:

---

[100] W. K. C. Guthrie, *The Sophists*, (Cambridge: Cambridge University Press, 1971) p. 34.

[101] Plato, Meno 91b.

[102] Plato, Sophist 235a.

[103] Plato, Sophist 231c-e.

[104] Xenophon, Memorabilia I.6.13 cited by W.K. C. Guthrie, The Sophists, p. 36.

[105] Aristotle, De Sophisticis Elenchis 165a20-23.

The Sophist belonged to no organization, nor did they all share a common body of specific belief…and they founded no schools, either in the sense of academic institutions or in that of groups of individuals committed to the promulgation of specific philosophical doctrines.[106]

Though there was no agreed body of ideas to be imparted into the desiring youths of Athens, there are some characteristics so general that they constitute the essence of who they were and are: teaching of virtue (virtue is a term that englobes so many other crafts) and charging fees for what they teach. As we have seen the first part of their essential characteristics, let us try to substantiate the second claim.

Plato tells us that Protagoras was one of the best teachers of culture and virtue, and the first to announce himself to the Greeks by the name of Sophist and "the first to claim payment for this service."[107] Emphasizing that Protagoras was the first to claim fee for rendering a service of this nature could have shocked Plato who knew that many eminent professionals in Athens did what these guys came to do without charging fees. So, we could say that fees were the major driving force behind the availability of these itinerant teachers. The names of Gorgias of Leontini, Prodicus of Ceos and Hippias of Elis are mentioned as men capable of going into any city and actually persuading young men to leave the company of their fellow citizens and attach themselves to them for a certain amount of money.[108] Euthydemus and Dionysodorous are mentioned as men capable of teaching anyone who would pay the fee, no age and no brains barred—all welcome, all would easily learn their clever system.[109] Plato in the *Sophist* describes this class of people who profess to form acquaintances only for the sake of virtue and demand a reward in the shape of money as the Sophists.[110] Their stock in trade was speech making and speech delivering, and money making.

---

[106] C. C. W. Taylor, "Introduction" *in Routledge History of Philosophy*, vol. I. From the Beginning to Plato, edited by C. C. W. Taylor, (London: Routeledge, 1997), p. 5.

[107] Plato, Protagoras 349a.

[108] Plato, Apology 19e-20a.

[109] Plato, Euthydemus 304b-c.

[110] Plato, Sophist 223a.

## 2. The Tools in the Sophists' Armoury:

When we say tools, we mean the common means or characteristics which enable the Sophists to achieve their purported goal of getting adherents to themselves and making them willing preys of exploitation. One of the most potent tools in their armoury is **rhetoric.**

Though all the Sophists practiced rhetoric, the Sophist who was an expert in this art of rhetoric was Gorgias of Leontini.[111] He could make rhetoricians of his students. As the best of the public speakers of his day, Gorgias delineates that in simple sense rhetoric is an art which secures its effects through 'the use of words.'[112] To confirm this interest in the use of words, Broadie gives them exceptional recognition for bringing human interest on the nature of the human *logos*:

> The Sophists were pioneers of systematic reflection on the nature of human *logos* (which variously means 'speech,' 'language,' 'argument,' 'reason'). They worked for control of the power of *logos* in the interest of familiar objectives, but they also rode with it into an entire new space of intellectual possibility. The key element of this brave new world was awareness of human mentality as a force with its own nature and laws of development, which moulds itself by means of its products, namely culture and institutions.[113]

It is by the art of rhetoric that the Sophists especially Gorgias, realized the power of the human person over his *logos* and the power of the *logos* over the human person. Broadie calls this double realization "the fundamental insight of the sophists."[114] Plato reporting Gorgias notes that this art that employs the *logos* gives man freedom in general and dominion over others.[115] While Gorgias may not be said to have desired

---

[111] Plato, Gorgias 449a.

[112] Ibid. 450e.

[113] Sarah Broadie, "The Sophists and Socrates," Ibid., p. 75.

[114] Sarah Broadie, Ibid.

[115] Plato, Gorgias 452d.

rhetoric as a means of power over others, some other Sophists actually did use it for the exploitation of others and for the pursuit of other sinister motives. Thrasymachus, Polus, Callicles, etc fall within this bracket. Though documentation may fail us, we still know that the "whole teaching of the Sophists is summed up in the art of rhetoric."[116]

Rhetoric functions by persuasion and as result is not very much interested in the truth than in what appears to be the case. Truth and knowledge are all mere illusions as what is more probable deserves more respect than truth.[117] It goes without saying that when the objective is to impress or persuade, there is the concomitant effect of insincerity and exaggeration. The purpose and not truth is what counts: get the adherent or the hearer to do my bidding. Hence Plato notes that the art and substance of rhetoric is to produce persuasion in the soul of the hearer.[118] What are the effects of such persuasion in the soul? One of such is dominion over others:

> I mean the power to convince by your words the judges in court, the senators in Council, the people in the Assembly, or in any other gathering of a citizen body. And yet possessed of such power you will make the doctor, you will make the trainer your slave, and your businessman will prove to be making money, not for himself, but for another, for you who can speak and persuade multitudes.[119]

How true this is will be seen in our verification of this method in the Pentecostal churches of Nigeria.

Another major tool in their armoury is the **teaching of areté**:

This 'virtue' has been a recurrent part of our write up on the Sophists. It is very important because that's exactly what they claim to do and how they identify themselves: teachers of *areté*. Though

---

[116] W. K. C. Guthrie, *The Sophists*, (Cambridge: Cambridge University Press, 1971), p. 20.

[117] Plato, Phaedrus 267a.

[118] Plato, Gorgias 453a.

[119] Ibid. 452e.

translations take *areté* to be virtue, it is generally agreed that this virtue or excellence is not restricted to just moral or ethical virtue of rightness.

> *Areté* when used without qualification denoted those qualities of human excellence which made a man a natural leader in his community, and hitherto it had been believed to depend on certain natural or even divine gifts which were the mark of good birth and breeding.[120]

They are sets of skills or abilities needed for success in public life. But inquiring whether these virtues or excellences were teachable was a frequent topic for Plato and his interlocutors. If they were teachable, could one allow that task to be carried out by the Sophists with some form of payment? To all of the questions Plato had major doubts and for some serious reasons.

Socrates went out to verify the knowledge which these professionals claimed to possess and to his greatest surprise, he found out that they were not really good. In fact, "it seemed to me, as I pursued my investigation at the god's command, that the people with the greatest reputations were almost entirely deficient, while others who were supposed to be their inferiors were much better qualified in practical intelligence."[121] So what then did they teach for fees when they were ignorant of their claims? It was highly contested whether virtue was even teachable. Experience in Athens proved that young men learnt such *areté* by living with the family members and copying their ways of life and tradition. The excellent professionals of earlier epoch like Pericles, never inculcated virtues into his boys nor gave them out to be instructed by another. They were simply left to "browse around on their own like sacred cattle, on the chance of picking up virtue automatically."[122] In the case of a child in need of the *areté* imparted by the professionals—Sophists, Socrates suggested to Anytus that he would be sending his visitor Meno to them. This suggestion was met with serious criticism from Anytus. As reported by Plato:

---

[120] W. K. C. Guthrie, The Sophists, p. 25.

[121] Plato, Apology 22a.

[122] Plato, Protagoras 319e-320b.

> Good heavens, what a thing to say ! I hope no relative of
> mine or any of my friends, Athenian or foreign, would be
> so mad as to go and let himself be ruined by those people.
> That is what they are, the manifest ruin and corruption
> of anyone who comes into contact with them.[123]

If they were real professionals in their chosen task of teaching virtue, how could association with them be described in such unpalatable language as "manifest ruins and corruption of anyone who comes into contact with them"? But the educational terrain of Athens at the epoch encouraged the arrival of these Sophists and the flocking of the youths to them. To Hippocrates who desired to be educated by the Sophist Protagoras, he was warned to weigh the risk before doing so: going to Protagoras was compared to entrusting one's soul to the care of another without knowing the ability of this other to care for the soul. That venture according to Socrates would only portend imminent danger to what is most precious to the individual—the soul.[124]

The last tool in the armoury of the Sophists is **sophistry**:

> At the epoch of the ancient Sophists, "sophistry" had no distinct line of difference with "rhetoric." Both were equivalent to each other. However, with the knowledge that rhetorics is not intrinsically negative, it is becoming clearer and clearer that sophistry is not equivalent to rhetoric. While the latter has been described as the art of persuasion using the human *logos*, the former—sophistry—is now frequently used to denote the negative use of rhetorics for manipulative purposes. Gorgias the rhetorician confirms to us that sophistry can employ the human *logos* for any unsavoury purpose, and make itself more important than even experts in the selected field could be.[125] Gorgias enumerates that he had had the occasion to convince patients more than doctors and surgeons—experts in the medical field, to accept his counsel by no other power other than rhetoric. This is a clear example of where a charlatan in possession of sophistry could be taken seriously more than

---

[123] Plato, Meno 91b-c.

[124] Plato, Protagoras 313a-b.

[125] Plato, Gorgias 456a-d.

a professional. Does this not agitate our minds why charlatans and tricksters in motor parks and buses across Nigeria persuade people into buying fake drugs for original and paying for their safe-journey-prayers on daily basis? Some of them that are courageous, move up the ladder by packaging themselves better, opening up churches and with Bibles in hand, begin hypnotizing people into becoming their slaves and emptying their bank accounts for the Pastors' projects?

## 3. Pentecostal Churches in Nigeria as Fields of Sophistry

Pentecostalism is a phenomenon or a renewal movement in the Christian churches which emphasizes personal encounter with God in Jesus Christ through the baptism of the Holy Spirit. It has been traced to the outpour of the Holy Spirit on the apostles with the attendant gift of speaking in tongues (Acts 2). The Churches with these characteristics are termed Pentecostal Churches. According to Ihejirika:

> Within the Nigerian context, the term Pentecostalism refers to Protestant Christian denominations which emphasise salvation by faith in the atoning death of Jesus Christ through personal conversion and the authority of Scripture in matters of faith and Christian practice, and a stress on the signs of the Spirit's radical transforming power, especially the Pentecostal signs of faith healing, and speaking in tongues.[126]

Though they do not have uniform body of doctrine like the main Christian churches—Catholic and Anglican—do, they hold on to the possibility of experiencing the gift of the tongues. Their rise to prominence has been attributed to the rising poverty in the country just like the Athenian city of the fifth century had needs for professional teachers of excellence to usher the Athenian youths into the future. Pentecostal Churches positioned themselves as the bastion of hope to the spiritual and physical problems of the poor Nigerian masses, with their pie-in-the-sky prosperity messages.[127] We shall try to elucidate

---

[126] Walter C. Ihejirika, *From Catholicism to Pentecostalism*, (Enugu: Snaap Press Ltd, 2006), p. 2.

[127] Nkechi C. Rotimi et al., "Nigerian Pentecostal Churches and Their

some concrete instances of doctrines where they employ their power of Sophistic rhetorics at its devastating effect for the financial exploitation of their numerous adherents.

## 4. The Common Themes of Pentecostal Services:

Like the Sophists of fifth century Athens, Pentecostal Churches in Nigeria under the direction of their various pastors, do not all share a common body of specific belief. There are however some distinctive themes that run across most of their religious teachings for the simple reason that they are themes particular with the needs of the poor masses who adhere to them. These themes include: prosperity, miraculous healing, wait and take evangelism or conversion, and neutralization of witchcraft.[128] They are in general terms the special areas of expertise which belong to the family of the teachable *areté* of these modern-day Sophists. For the administration of these excellences, the adherents of these pastors would have to offer huge sums of money.

### a. Prosperity Gospel:

This is essentially the message that God does not want you to be poor but that he has destined riches, good health, wealth for his children. The Pentecostal Pastor generally held to be one of the pioneer preachers of prosperity message in Nigeria is David O. Oyedepo. As he writes in his book:

> Why then do you think that your lack excites God? Which father is excited to see his children begging all around? Have you ever heard somebody give a testimony saying: "I thank God, two of my sons are beggars?" Your children's children will never beg! I want you to know that the prosperity God has planned for you has nothing to do with your profession, your career or your family background.[129]

---

Prosperity Messages: A Safeguard Against Poverty in Nigeria," Mgbakoigba *Journal of African Studies* Vol.5, No. 2, June 2016, p. 10.

[128] Fred A. Amadi, "Understanding the Practices that Define Pentecostal Christianity in Nigeria," *European Scientific Journal*, Nov. 2013, p. 297.

[129] David O. Oyedepo, *Understanding Financial Prosperity* (Ikeja: Dominion

Nobody in the world actually prays to be materially poor or even rejoices in poverty of a material kind. To make prosperity as the central message of the gospel is off the mark. If prosperity is actually the ultimate sign of God's blessing, why did the incarnate Son of God—Jesus Christ—live in poverty, with a poor family, all his earthly existence? Pentecostal Pastors will never address this issue because like all Sophists, the most important thing is not the truth but winning arguments and persuading people into accepting one set of appearance over another. This is sophistry at its best as it makes use of persuasion in producing belief in people without knowledge. It is very persuasive but not instructive about right and wrong.[130] This message encourages tithing and continuous donation by church members to the Pastors' projects. In so many of the Pentecostal churches, offerings take place immediately after the people have been worked up by the means of rhetoric. They are made to believe that the more you give the more you will receive riches in abundance. Where on earth does it happen that if you give your riches away, you receive more of those riches in return?

**b. The Quest for Miraculous Healing:**
The quest for miraculous healing of bodily and spiritual ailments is another of the common themes marking the Pentecostal churches of Nigeria. Everybody aims at and enjoys good health of mind and body. Nobody is pleased when he finds that he has become incapable or dependent because of illness. In the scriptures, Jesus went about doing good and healing the sick. But we know that healing of the sick is not something that happens at one's beck and call and in fact it does rarely happen especially when God deems fit. The frequency with which Pentecostal Pastors claim to be healing sick people has become quite embarrassing for every right-thinking person. Most of these healings are claimed to take place during prayer crusades organized for self publicity and financial enrichment. No wonder the overemphasis on healing activities. Instead of advising and helping people to seek medical attention in the hospitals, some Pentecostal ministers persuade their followers to seek miracles, signs and wonders. Have they become

Publishers, 1997), p. 7.

[130] Plato, Protagoras 455a.

ignorant of the warning by Jesus for those unnecessarily searching for miracles and wonders? "Why do this generation demand for a sign? I tell you solemnly no sign shall be given to this generation except the sign of Jonah" (Mk 8:11-13).

The continuous quest for miracles is part of the prosperity gospel that denies the place of the cross and suffering in the life of a Christian. By implication, it negates the salvific importance of the cross—suffering and death, as preludes to glory.

**c. Wait and Take Evangelism or Conversion:**
This is very characteristic of Pentecostal churches in Nigeria. This form of evangelism harps on the conversion experience that instantly transforms one from darkness into light. Your past experiences no longer matter once you proclaim that 'Jesus is your personal Lord and Saviour.' That is an example of the Pentecostal rhetoric that creates a conviction that is persuasive without being instructive. It was Gorgias that gave us two types of persuasion: persuasion that produces belief without knowledge and the persuasion that produces knowledge without belief.[131] In religious assemblies, it is the persuasion that produces belief without knowledge that is in vogue. Another of such is the promise of being 'Born again.' You begin to enjoy salvation and direct access to God once you accept to be "born again."

> Being "born again" can be easy and in that sense it seems to be a relief. Once one accepts Christ as one's personal Lord and Saviour, the past may not necessarily cease to exist, but it does not matter at all.[132]

The base for this may be traced to the biblical passage of John 3:3 where Nicodemus encountering Jesus Christ learnt that unless one is born again of water and the holy spirit, he will not see the kingdom of God. Interpretations of this nature are only but literal. The truth that Pentecostal Pastors will never tell their adherents out of ignorance or in consistency with the essence of their profession—making gains—is

---

[131] Plato, Gorgias 454e.

[132] D. Oyesola, "Fundamentalism and the Catholic Faith in Nigerian Higher Institutions" (Iperu-Remo: Ambassador Publications, 1994), p. 7. This reference appeared in Pentecostalism: Proceedings of the National Seminaries Committee Workshop, Jos, 2004, edited by Charles M. Hammawa, (Jos: Fab Anieh Ltd, 2005), p. 35.

that true conversion involves a "reformation of character." This would involve personal effort over a span of months.

### d. Neutralization of Witchcraft:

The ability to neutralize witchcraft is another of the *areté* that Pentecostal ministers claim to be experts in. Witchcraft is part of the Nigerian indigenous religious worldview which believes that human beings can be agents for the malicious works of demons. Where ignorance reigns and there is so much belief in superstitions more than reality, belief in witchcraft thrives. Road accidents, lack of electricity, deaths in families, are normally seen as results of some demonic attacks from perceived and imagined enemies. "Spiders, cobwebs, cockroaches, wall geckos or any creeping insects are seen as demons due to the kind of things you teach them in church."[133] Failure of social services to be provided by the government is completely exonerated. Instead of encouraging their faithfuls "to keep their surroundings clean, they are busy binding and screaming Holy Ghost fire at the insects around them."[134] It is in this worldview that Pentecostals tap into, amplify the phenomenon and present themselves as powerful enough to solve. The Catholic Bishops have addressed this issue thus:

> Seeing demons where there are none, blaming them for all troubles, having obsessive fear of them, and preaching about them excessively, are marks of a superstitious trend that does not find support in Christian tradition.[135]

The Pentecostal ministers know that this practice is not part of the Christian tradition; but if it can be exploited for personal aggrandizement, then it is justifiable. That is the essence of sophistry—

---

[133] Amaka Nicholas, "Things Nigerian Pastors Should Stop Doing," Saturday Sun, Vol. 16, No. 844, March 2, 2019, p. 17.

[134] Ibid.

[135] Guidelines for the Healing Ministry in the Catholic Church Issued by the Catholic Bishops Conference of Nigeria, 1999 in P. Schneller (ed). *The Voice of the Voiceless*, (Lagos: CBCN Publications 2002), p. 344.

using clever but false argumentative persuasions with the intention of deceiving the gullible. This is why Plato describes them as "manifest ruins and corruption of anyone who comes into contact with them."[136]

## 5. The Effects of the Activities of the Religious Sophists in Nigeria

In Athens, the Sophists tended to be exerting only positive influences on the Athenian society until a philosopher in the guise of Plato studied them and exposed them for what they truly were—real fraudsters. The effects in Athens of the epoch can be assimilated to the effects in Nigeria of the modern-day Sophists in religious garb. Let us examine *Protagoras* 313c-314b passage.

Exposing oneself to the influence of the Sophists is like exposing one's soul to danger. Sophists are like merchants or peddlers of the goods by which a soul is nourished. They sell all sorts of goods they have in their wares without knowing exactly which is harmful or beneficial to the soul. They praise all their goods and sell them indiscriminately to equally ignorant buyers who happen to be their followers. If these goods were provisions or eatables, you would still have a chance in that you could store them away and get the advice of experts as to the suitability of eating them or not and the quantity or quality to consume. Compared to knowledge, the risk of buying is greater. This is because knowledge goes directly into the soul and you may not have the opportunity to store it away and consult before consuming it.

> When you have paid for it, you must receive it straight into the soul. You go away having learned it and are benefitted or harmed accordingly.[137]

The solution which Socrates proposes is that only those who are experts in such wares should buy them. But in a situation where the majority of buyers are ignorant, the only thing it assures is the continuity of the business and the continuous destruction of the souls of the ignorant buyers. That is exactly the general description of what is happening in Nigeria.

---

[136] Plato, Meno 91c.

[137] Plato, Protagoras 314b.

One of the major effects of the activities of the Sophists in religious garb in Nigeria is **the bastardization of the moral fiber of the Nigerian society**. How the people react depends much on the influences they are subjected to. The rhetorics that enable the pastors to turn the Bible into a major instrument of deception must be highlighted. Rhetorics bring about persuasion of the crowd but never to convince people of the truth. It is rhetoric that enables the Pentecostal Pastors to frame the Biblical passages in order "to shore up the key teachings in Nigeria's Pentecostal message."[138] An example is the interpretation of *Galatians* 6:7 "A person will reap exactly what he sows." It is a passage that encourages the practice of good works as a solid foundation for eternal salvation. But for the Pentecostal Pastors, it is a passage that justifies the practice of seed sowing in the church for material blessings from God. Your reward would depend on the largeness of your heart and your financial donation to the church. Thus, instead of preaching salvation, they persuade their followers into contributing to the financial wellbeing of the pastor and his Church. Where the Bible message should be talking about salvation, the Pentecostal Pastor has made it to be talking of materialism.[139] What we get here is a clear case of throwing aside objectivity for relativism where one can decide for oneself what the truth is. When people create their own moral standards, the society is in trouble. Those who encourage seed sowing with the preface of God's abundant blessings on the sower, inevitably encourage ill-gotten wealth. Stories abound of many Christians who steal from their places of work in order to meet with the obligation of tithing and sowing seed for God's blessings in return.[140]

Fortunately, some of the Sophists on the level of pedagogy promoted relativism. Protagoras has been singled out as the father of relativism when he wrote and taught that 'Man is the measure of all

---

[138] Fred A. Amadi, "Understanding the Practices that Define Pentecostal Christianity in Nigeria," *European Scientific Journal*, Vol. 9, No. 32, 2013, p. 304.

[139] Ibid.

[140] Cf B. Johnson, "The Pastorpreneur's Fresh Scandal," *The News*, Dec. 20, 2010, pp. 18-22 cited in Fred A. Amadi, "Understanding the Practices that Define Pentecostal Christianity in Nigeria," p. 299.

things; of things that are that they are and things that are not, that they are not.' When followers who are not strong in differentiating what actually is real from illusion are constantly fed a message of this nature, the result is that they eventually lose faith in the power of reason and in the power of truth. According to Guthrie:

> Rhetorical teaching was not confined to form and style, but dealt also with the substance of what was said. How could it fail to inculcate the belief that all truth was relative and no one knew anything for certain?[141]

In real life situations, people subjected to this become very weak in the face of moral decisions. The guiding principle would no longer be what is true, but rather what the end that I want is.

It is this same principle that is at the foundation of the prosperity gospel which is the mainstream belief of the Pentecostal churches in Nigeria. This is the gospel that is gradually **destroying the authentic Christian tradition and faith** in the power of the cross and solidifying the dissemination of falsehood. Those who consistently reject the cross as not their portion, and sickness and poverty as not their portion, will inevitably, perhaps by ignorance or bad leadership, also reject the narrow gate that leads to salvation. Prosperity gospel teaches that suffering is not a part of Christianity, that God has ordained riches, wealth, and open doors for his children. Regardless of whatever one may believe, I think that the true colour of prosperity gospel is heresy because it denies that salvation is wrought by Christ through the cross. Did Christ the Lord not specify: "If you want to be a follower of mine, carry your cross everyday and follow me" (Mk 8:34)? Does whoever rejects this not reject the foundation of Christian teaching? Another reason why prosperity gospel is wrong is that it is comparable to the gate of hell. In *Mt 7:13*, Jesus Christ the Lord again specifies:

> Go in through the narrow gate because the gate to hell is wide and the road that leads to it is easy, and there are many who travel it.

---

[141] W. K.C. Guthrie, The Sophists, p. 51.

Be that as it may, do the Pentecostal Pastors who pride in being acute readers of the Bible, not come across these capital passages on which the authentic Christian faith depends? Unless they do selective reading and interpretation of passages they manipulate for their selfish ends. That is exactly what rhetorics do—not concerned with the truth but with manipulating people to suit a certain goal. Gorgias the master rhetorician tells us the effects of rhetorics:

> And yet possessed of such power you will make the doctor, you will make the trainer your slave, and your businessman will prove to be making money, not for himself, but for another, for you who can speak and persuade multitudes.[142]

Another effect that is even becoming alarming now is **the frequent establishment of Churches** almost on weekly basis in every nook and cranny of the Nigerian street. In the Western world, industries are the main powers driving their economy and assimilating many of their qualified but unemployed citizens. In Nigeria today, the fastest growing industry is the Pentecostal contraptions that go by the name of Churches. Many dropouts from schools, many unsuccessful businesspeople easily find their way into the Pentecostal church industries. What could be the major motivation for them if not the riches easily accumulated by the colleague pastors within very short periods? Once they learn the art of deception in the name of God, they carry their Bibles and quickly turn open shops or rooms into Pentecostal Churches. They claim to be seeing visions, prophesying and healing all sorts of ailments and diseases. A Nigerian who feels concerned by this unhealthy trend writes:

> Dear men of God, you need to go get yourselves gainfully employed, acquire a skill or learn a trade and stop opening new churches every day. The fact that you can see visions and predict future events doesn't mean you should start your own church.[143]

---

[142] Plato, Gorgias 452e.

[143] Amaka Nicholas, "Things Nigerian Pastors Should Stop Doing," *Saturday Sun*, Vol. 16, No. 844, March 2, 2019, p. 17.

As true as the simple admonition could be, what Nicholas fails to understand is that those men and women have acquired a skill and learnt a trade that have given them a gainsome employment in an environment where such employment thrives. The number of Pentecostal churches in Nigeria has exploded that it will really be an exercise in utility trying to make a guess work.[144] The frequency with which they are exploding in number tells you that the environment in which they thrive perhaps demands them. Over and above all, they are making a hale of fortune out of the ignorance of their teeming followers. Does it surprise anybody that they are stupendously rich? Not in the least when we remember that the original Sophists were very rich. Protagoras earned more money from his being a Sophist than an excellent craftsman like Phidias and ten other sculptors put together.[145] Gorgias and Prodicus were wealthier than the practitioners of any other art.[146] Pentecostal Pastors are among the wealthiest men in Nigeria as of today. Some of them fly in private jets and drive sleezy cars. But most of those they exploit live in squalor and find it difficult meeting the elementary needs for survival. In the final analysis, these Sophists in religious garb are, in the language of Socrates's interlocutor Callicles, "worthless people."[147]

## 6. How Do We Solve A Problem Like Sophists?

Philosophy in its essence is not problem-solving oriented. What it does is to analyse situations of things, understand them and expose them in their true reality. That is exactly what we have tried to do in this write-up.

The solution that may be remarkably effective in Nigeria will be political if the complexities of a hydra-headed country like ours permit. One of the major reasons why Pentecostalism and their false messages of hope attract and keep attracting many poor people is the lack of elementary services. If majority of Nigerians are properly educated, they would resist anybody who would try to intellectually deceive them

---

[144] Walter C. Ihejirika, *From Catholicism to Pentecostalism*, (Enugu: Snaap Press Ltd, 2006), p. 3.

[145] Plato, Meno 91d.

[146] Plato, Greater Hippias 281b-d.

[147] Plato, Gorgias 520a.

into the state of religious slavery. Unfortunately, it is a long way before our educational institution is what it should be.

Socrates talks of the need to acquire moral goodness. This virtue is particularly important in our country for the Pentecostal Pastors and for the masses thronging after them. The first and chief concern for everyone is "not for your bodies nor for your possessions, but for the highest welfare of your souls…wealth does not bring goodness, but goodness brings wealth and every other blessing, both to the individual and to the state."[148]

Proliferation can only be curtailed by some form of strict control. The rate at which things are going in this country, it may reach a point where it would require the intervention of the government (where we have one) to sanitize the society. As radical as it may seem, Rwandan government had formerly closed 5000 churches and has increased the number to 8000. One of the major conditions for closure is lack of authentic theological certificate from a recognised theological institute. Some Pastors in this country are quacks who are into the industry to make money and nothing else. How can they not be perpetrators and promoters of crimes? Because the government fails in her duty to provide or create jobs, people are quickly seeing visions and becoming prophets. If adequate jobs are available, most people would go off the Pentecostal industry for good. An additional solution for this religious menace in Nigeria would be to establish stricter rules and enforce them. But can corruption ever allow such rules to work in Nigeria?

---

[148] Plato, Apology 30a-b.

# Bibliography

Amadi, Fred A. "Understanding the Practices that Define Pentecostal Christianity in Nigeria," *European Scientific Journal*, Vol. 9, No. 32, 2013.

Blackson, Thomas A. *Ancient Greek Philosophy: From the Presocratics to the Hellenistic Philosophers*, (West-Sussex: Wiley-Blackwell, 2011).

Broadie, S. "The Sophists and Socrates" in *The Cambridge Companion to Greek and Roman Philosophy* (Cambridge: Cambridge University Press, 2003).

Guthrie, W. K. C. *The Sophists*, (Cambridge: Cambridge University Press, 1971).

Hammawa, Charles M. *(ed). Pentecostalism: Proceedings of the National Seminaries Committee Workshop*, Jos, 2004, (Jos: Fab Anieh Ltd, 2005).

Ihejirika, Walter C. *From Catholicism to Pentecostalism*, (Enugu: Snaap Press Ltd, 2006).

Johnson, B. "The Pastorpreneur's Fresh Scandal," The News, Dec. 20, 2010.

Kenny, A. *A New History of Western Philosophy*, (Oxford: Clarendon Press, 2010).

Kerferd, G. B. *The Sophistic Movement*, (Cambridge: Cambridge University Press, 1981).

Nicholas, A. "Things Nigerian Pastors Should Stop Doing," *Saturday Sun*, Vol. 16, No. 844, March 2, 2019.

Oyedepo, David O. *Understanding Financial Prosperity* (Ikeja: Dominion Publishers, 1997).

Oyesola, D. "Fundamentalism and the Catholic Faith in Nigerian Higher Institutions" (Iperu-Remo: Ambassador Publications, 1994).

Plato, *The Collected Dialogues of Plato*, edited by Hamilton and Huntington Cairns, (New Jersey: Princeton University Press, 1989).

Rotimi, Nkechi C. et al., "Nigerian Pentecostal Churches and Their Prosperity Messages: A Safeguard Against Poverty in Nigeria," *Mgbakoigba Journal of African Studies* Vol. 5, No. 2, June 2016.

Schneller, P. (ed). *The Voice of the Voiceless*, (Lagos: CBCN Publications 2002).

Taylor, C. C. W. (ed). *Routledge History of Philosophy*, vol. I. *From the Beginning to Plato* (London: Routeledge, 1997).

# Chapter 8

## The Transcendental Primordial Values of the Human Society vis-à-vis the Nigerian State

Chrysanthus Nnaemeka Ogbozo


**Abstract**

Most cultures or peoples appreciate their belongingness to the human society. One of the ways of manifesting such appreciation is to give big and nice names to their countries or towns. For instance, countries like Britain and Serbia assign themselves the adjective 'Great': 'Great Britain', 'Great Serbia'. On the level of town, we know many of them who prefer to call themselves the "ancient kingdom" of so and so place. All these positive appraisals underline the pride and joy of belongingness to one country/town or another. Beneath the positive appraisals are some perceived 'values' which a country or town wants to project as their *raison d'être*. Therefore, this paper argues that though a state may have begun spontaneously in a natural way as Aristotle once described,[149] still the state cannot endure or survive as a social institution unless it is founded on some primordial values that have transcendental outlook. Such survival, many have speculated, seems to be eluding Nigeria amid unprecedented phenomena being witnessed in the society today. This paper is, therefore, ethically and metaphysically oriented.


**Introduction**

It is a fact that nobody chooses the place of his birth, but he simply finds himself in a family and in a particular society, and from there, begins his initial socialization. Aristotle noted this fact many years ago

---

[149] Cf. Aristotle Politics, Bk 1, 1252 b: 'several villages coming together to a single community in such a way that it becomes self-sufficing and hence called state'.

when he wrote that "when several villages are united in a single complete community, large enough to be nearly or quite self-sufficing, the state comes into existence".[150] Elsewhere I had maintained that the cited text underlines two elements: first, it depicts the birth of a state by the coming together of several small units. Secondly, it highlights the need for the state to be self-sufficing.[151] Given this natural pulsation in man to form a larger unit called state, Aristotle further maintains that "man is by nature a political animal, and that he who by nature and not by mere accident is without a state, is either a bad man or above humanity; he is like the tribeless, lawless, heartless one…"[152] But more than the foregoing spontaneous aggregation of small units to form a state, Aristotle signals a more superior force in the formation and survival of a society when he observed as follows:

> Every state is a community of some kind, and every community is established with a view to *some good*; for everyone always acts in order to obtain that which they think good. But if communities aim at *some good*, the state or political community, which is the highest of all, and which embraces all the rest, aims at *good in a greater degree* than any other, and at *the highest good*.[153]

It is noteworthy to observe the many references to the good in the cited passage. In Aristotelian view, the human society exists simply for the cultivation and promotion of the good of all, but of course, according to different classes in the society. In a sense, 'the good' becomes the standard of any value that an individual or a group in a society is pursuing.

Against this backdrop of natural and social constitutions of a society which, above all, anchors on the good, one is baffled to behold different kinds of strange pursuits posing as values in the Nigerian society of

---

[150] Ibid.,

[151] Ike Obiora & Chidiebere Onyia, (eds.), *Ethics in Higher Education: Foundations for Sustainable Development*, vol. 2 (Geneva: Globethics, 2018), 308.

[152] Aristotle, Politics, Bk. I, 1253a.

[153] Aristotle, Politics, Bk. I, 1252a. The bold stress is mine.

today. The scenarios from different quarters present us with the following pictures:

(a) Educationally, the common test of someone who is educated in today's Nigeria is a mere presentation of certificates, a situation that labels our type of education, "certificate-education".

(b) Politically, the constant shameful dramas of sharing monies and using security apparatus for intimidation before and during elections have become a commonplace phenomenon.

(c) On the level of governance, there are eloquent signs of nepotism, tribalism and sectionalism which overthrow merit, and enthrone mediocrity and inefficiency.

(d) On the religious sphere, many self-styled "men of God" have taken the stage, preaching all sorts of gospel of popularity and prosperity, and worse, employing fetish and occult means in the name and the power of the Christian God.

These scenarios show the depth and velocity by which the primordial values are vanishing from the Nigerian society. The situation calls for a re-assessment of values, and particularly the foundational ones. To be methodological, such re-assessment can take off with a consideration of the question – What is value and its nature?

**The Concept of Value: Meaning, Brief History and Characteristics**
First of all, the term "value" has a dual meaning: 'verb' and 'noun-meanings'. As a verb, 'to value' refers to "a certain mental act or attitude of valu*ing* or valua*tion*", whereas as a noun, it may be used in an abstract or concrete form.[154] Abstractly, Baylis maintains that the word 'value'

---

[154] Cf. Charles A. Baylis, "Value", in Dagobert D. Runes, *Dictionary of Philosophy*, rev. & enlarged ed., (NY: Rowmann and Allanheld, 1984), 346. See

designates "the property of value or being valuable" and hence, it is interchangeable with the words "worth" and "goodness". On the concrete level, the term points to 'things that exhibit the properties of value or things that are valued'.

A further understanding of the meaning and nature of value can be seen from Frankena's historical survey of the concept. He opines that the concept has, from the time of Plato, been considered under different concepts which, *inter-alia*, include the following: "the good, the end, the right, obligation, virtue, moral judgment, aesthetic judgment, the beautiful, truth and validity".[155] Frankena makes two important observations after listing those cognate concepts of value. The first is that those cognate terms resurfaced in the nineteenth century, appearing as questions that were essentially found in Plato. The second observation is that those listed concepts/cognate terms belong to the same family of value insofar as they pertain to value or concern themselves with "what ought to be" in contradistinction to that which exists in the present, or had existed in the past or will even exist in the future.[156] In other words, "what ought to be" is a standard that is a-temporal, not time-bound. Though the said cognate terms are not grouped under the general heading of value, they are, however, considered "parts of the general theory of value and valuation", and this theory is variously studied by such disciplines like economics, ethics, aesthetics, jurisprudence, education, and somehow by logic and epistemology.[157]

It is equally important to underline the extension of the meaning of value in contemporary times. Again, according to Frankena, the term has meaning which is diffused from economics to philosophy and from there to the social sciences.[158] The original meaning of the term in

also: Wikipedia on "Instrumental and Intrinsic Value".

[155] Cf. William K. Frankena, "Value and Valuation" in Paul Edwards, ed., *The Encyclopedia of Philosophy*, Vol. 8, (New York: Macmillan Pub. Co. Inc & The Free Press, 1967), 229.

[156] Ibid.,

[157] Ibid.

[158] Ibid.

contemporary times is said to have been limited to 'the worth of a thing', where the word "worth" is understood in economic terms. Consequently, a first extension of the meaning of the term finds its *locus* in the field of economics and in what has come to be called the "theory of value". From economics, the concept of value got introduced into philosophy with broader meanings that were championed by some German philosophers like Rudolf Hermann, Lotze, Albrecht Ritschl and Nietzsche.[159]

Within the ambient of the philosophical employment of the term, Frankena speaks of diversities in meaning. And before examining some opinions of philosophers, his X-ray shows that there are two major senses of the concept in a philosophical setting. Those senses are 'the narrow' and 'wide meanings' of the term. In a narrow sense, 'value' denotes "the good", "the desirable" and "the worthwhile" whereas a wider sense of the term is when it is used to refer to those qualities he mentioned earlier like virtue, truth, beauty, holiness, etc.[160] Regarding the views of contemporary philosophers on the concept, Frankena further notes that the pursuit of a general theory of value reached maturation in the works of two Austrian philosophers and disciples of Franz Brentano. The disciples in question are Alexius Meinong and Christian von Ehrenfels. As it were, these disciples somehow generated interest in value-question among philosophers like Max Scheler and Nicolai Hartmann – two philosophers who followed the phenomenological footsteps of Edmund Husserl. It is expected that the concept of value for the disciples of Husserl would be largely phenomenological. But the situation would be different in Britain where the concept of value has been predominantly traditional i.e., associated with the concept of "good" or "right". In the British list then are persons like Bernard Bosanquet, John Mackenzie, John Laird and J. N. Findlay. Gradually, the interest in value theory heightened when its awareness reached the United States and with such thinkers like Hugo Münsterberg, Ralph Barton Perry, John Dewey, Paul W. Taylor championing its development.[161]

---

[159] Ibid.,

[160] Ibid.,

[161] Ibid.,

Furthermore, contributing to the question of characterizing value, De Finance gives us significant insight. Like Plato, De Finance maintains that *'the Good' moves the will* toward an activity. It does this through its two inseparable aspects called END and VALUE.[162] On the one hand, the *good is an end* in the sense of initiating the activity of the subject by drawing the subject to itself and making it tend toward it in an effort to capture it. On the other hand, *the good is value* (like a quality) that is found in an object. Put differently, the good as a moving activity is an end, and as a quality that is attracting a subject, it is a value. So the subject is the focus in terms of good or a desired end to be attained, but the good is also a quality in the object (concrete or abstract) which attracts the subject. De Finance further speaks of it in this way: 'the end is a defined good to which a subject tends toward whereas value is already some quality that is bestowed on a subject's activity'.[163] This being the case, De Finance maintains that both **"End"** and **"value"** are two inseparable aspects of the good. Nico Sprokel did underline these aspects as well but notes that a value is "a determined good for man; value is oriented toward man".[164]

By way of summary, it could be said that "the valuable" has come to be strongly identifiable with a whole lot of positive properties like 'goodness' or 'rightness' as well as the negative ones like evil, otherwise called "disvalue".[165]

At this juncture, it is necessary to examine some of the major characteristics of value in order to give a comprehensive picture of the meaning and appreciation of the valuable. A very basic trait of value which is very evident in the movement of the will toward the good is its *transcendental character.* As value is identifiable with **what ought to be** or **goodness/rightness**, it therefore remains the **"sought-after"** by humans. And even when value is acquired in a particular object or context in which it is found, it is not exhausted in that object/context.

---

[162] Joseph De Finance, *An Ethical Inquiry* (Roma: Editrice Pontificia Universita Gregoriana, 1991), 50 §17.

[163] Ibid.,

[164] Unpublished lectures on "The Good and the Values" at the Pontifical Gregorian University, Rome, 1991.

[165] Cf. Charles A. Baylis, "Value", 346.

For instance, the goodness that one feels when he drinks a glass of cold water on a very sunny day satisfies him quite well, but the cold water does not exhaust the goodness he enjoys by having a nice meal later or by taking a wonderful afternoon rest. This explanation on the transcendental nature of value leads one to a second characteristic of value, namely, its *interconnectedness with an object.* The value that moves the will is such that it is often linked to the existence of an object irrespective of whether the object is abstract or concrete. For instance, the desire to get education/knowledge (a kind of goodness) requires that one goes to school of any kind – academic, vocational, etc. A third feature of value was already noted above when we spoke of positive and negative value. In this section, we can articulate it as *the polarity of value.* That is to say, values are always paired or have two poles of positivity and negativity. While the positive is first defined in its direct contribution to the human society, the second is only defined as a lack of the positive. An additional trait could still be added in the name of *plurality of values.* As a matter of fact, we speak of values in plural. The plurality of values is also connected with the idea that values vary from place to place. In other words, what is valuable in one context may not count as a value in another context. This is because a lot of factors come into play in the determination of values, and the factors comprise of cultural, educational, weather and religious issues. The scope of this paper does not permit us to examine these factors. The much it allows us is to briefly consider some types of value.

**Types of Values**

Both Sprokel[166] and De Finance[167] speak of four types of values. Among them are firstly, what are called *infra-human* values. According to De Finance, this set of values are not precisely directed to man as such though can be appropriated by man. In his words, 'they are values of the sensory order'. In other words, they relate to what the senses agree to or disagree with, namely, the pleasant and the unpleasant.[168] In this set of values are included what he calls the *biological value*s as well.

---

[166] Niko Sprokel, "The Good and the Values", Unpublished Postgraduate Lectures, Gregorian University, Rome, 1990-92.

[167] Joseph De Finance, An Ethical Inquiry, 63-66.

[168] Ibid., 63.

De Finance speaks of biological values in two categories: objectively and subjectively. On the objective level, the concern is on values that favour health or sickness, and on the subjective level, values that have higher effects as they affect the interiority of the human person.

There is another type of values called *infra-moral or human values*: they are values that "involve the exercise of the powers of which are proper to man",[169] and hence can truly be called 'values meant for man'. De Finance identifies two sub-classes within this class of values: the first sub-class is *economic value* which determines either the prosperity or destitution of someone; success or failure of humans in many aspects, thereby contributing to their happiness or unhappiness. The importance of this set of values can further be seen from the point of view of the role that wealth and fame play in human society. De Finance says that the possession of wealth and fame affirms one's personality and are, to some extent, an extension of one's personality. For this reason, they are both good and desirable.[170] The second sub-class of human values are explained as spiritual values insofar as they are not primarily geared toward the satisfaction of biological needs. Some examples include truth which contrasts with falsehood, knowledge which is opposed to ignorance, beauty that contrasts with the ugly, peace/harmony that can be harmed by anarchy or disorder. These examples fall under what De Finance sub-classified with the terms – noetic, aesthetic, artistic and social values.[171]

In the third classification are *moral values*. According to De Finance, a moral value, usually spoken of in singular rather than in plural form 'affects the human person more intimately, especially in the exercise of his freedom'.[172] Given that the moral value is generally non-speculative, but directed toward making a judgment and decision, it is a value that is oriented toward the practical order, remarks De Finance. Given also that personal decision is often involved, moral value demands a good

---

[169] Ibid, 63.

[170] Ibid., 64.

[171] Ibid., 64.

[172] Ibid. 64.

dose of responsibility and often attracts the appraisal of the public. Categorically, De Finance says that this value gives the human person his true worth.[173] Much as De Finance's position sounds dogmatic on the supremacy of moral value over others, it is not difficult to see why he maintains such ground. This type of value is truly one of a valuation among values that majorly deal with pleasurable personal advantages. And because right reason is needed in the determination of this value, it does indeed confer considerable dignity to the human person.

The last class of values that Sprokel and De Finance discussed is *religious value*. This type of value shares some similarity with the former insofar as personal decision and commitment are often involved in both values. It might even be said that religious values hold more sway in their impact on the human individual than the earlier considered moral values. This is because religious values are strictly linked to a supreme being who is both the author of the subject making a decision for a particular value and the author of all values. According to De Finance, both moral and religious values are intimately linked, though religious ones are not to be reduced to the moral ones. Such link, he notes, shows that "morality cannot be perfect without religion, just as there can be no authentic religion without morality".[174] A note of caution has to be given here: that is to say, the position of De Finance has to be qualified. A morality that can be perfected by religion is a morality that can be critically discussed, and also a religion that is open to the changing signs of time i.e., a religion that takes into account the idea that the manifestations of revelation are ongoing. This comment on De Finance's position is necessary because of contemporary moralities and religions that have either dehumanized man or even killed humans in the name of 'holy doctrines' or 'special revelations'.

The foregoing exposition on types of value sets the stage for the consideration of the main thesis of this article, namely, that there are transcendental primordial values whose existence determines the other values.

---

[173] Ibid., 66.

[174] Ibid., 66.

## The Transcendence of the Primordial Values

The present discussion shall, first of all, identify those primordial or foundational values and then, in their exposition, try to show how transcendental the noted values are in the determination of other values, and with occasional references to the contemporary Nigerian attitudes to the said values.

The values in question here are inter-linked, either because of their conceptual affinity or because they have consequences that are connected to one another. We can distinguish three sets of primordial values which draw inspiration from the metaphysical discourse on the transcendental attributes of being. An exposition of those fundamental values now follows:

## (a) The Primordiality of Existence – Human Existence

From the days of Aristotle through the medieval era, especially in the philosophy of St. Thomas Aquinas and proceeding to the contemporary existential philosophy, there has been a strong emphasis on existence as a *fundamentum in rei*. The Aristotelian discourse on existence is largely theoretical in terms of the constitutive elements (i.e., existence and essence) of a finite entity. Though his exposition rested on such constitution, at different times, it is noteworthy to underline that his analyses show the fundamental nature of 'the act of to be' or 'existence'. Emerich underscores this point when he opines that the *'fact of existence'* is that which makes a thing to be real; it is therefore "an inner principle or ground of that which really is; *it is the inner ground through which beings are in themselves*".[175] To say that things are, because of this inner ground – 'act of to be', is to imply that that which occupies this position is a most primordial element in the universe of existents, and without it, there is simply nothingness. Hence, it surprises nobody when, in the contemporary era of philosophizing, some existentialists re-open the discussions on the subject, not from a theoretical or abstract standpoint, but from the perspective of the existentiality of existence. Even in the new existentialist discussions on the subject matter, the primacy of existence is all the more stressed, and sometimes in contradistinction

---

[175] Emerich Coreth Metaphysics, English ed by Joseph Donceel with a critique by B.J.F. Lonergan (New York: The Seabury Press, 1973), 79. The italics are mine.

to non-existence. For instance, Heidegger is known to have posed a question he called 'the question of all questions' and indeed, the fundamental question of metaphysics, namely: "why is there anything *at all* rather than nothing?"[176] In his own investigation into what is most basic in life, Jean Paul Sartre titled his major work – *Being and Nothingness* – which follows the trend of contrasting existence with non-existence.

To be noted in the elucidation of the primordiality of existence is the fact that it is equally transcendental in the traditional sense of that word. By the traditional notion of 'transcendence' is that which is not limited to any class or group but goes beyond every particularity in order to embrace all classes of things in the universe of all existents. In this way, the multiplicity of things that exist or can exist have just one common denominator, namely, 'existence'. Thus, existence is the common denominator that brings all things under one class (unus). Coreth formulates it better in this way: "insofar as something is, it is one, really identical with itself. Insofar as everything is, it is united with everything else… Being as being introduces no difference, no limit, no distinction. It posits pure identity and unity".[177] Given that existence is one with all things that exist, one can now understand why and how it is said that the attribute of existence is co-existence with and really identical with whatever is.[178] The implication which now stares at us here is this: if the universe of things must thrive, then the facticity of existence must be preserved or protected. This way of thinking is all the more valid for the lives of human beings who are known today to be the most intelligent beings on the surface of the planet Earth. It is therefore not

[176] Martin Heidegger, *An Introduction to Metaphysics*, trans. by Ralph Manheim (New York: Anchor Books, 1961), 1. I find the translation of Manheim here as the best among the English translations I have hitherto met because it is closest to the German original of the statement which is: "Warum ist <u>überhaupt</u> Seiendes und nicht vielmehr Nichts". The word "überhaupt" is often ignored in many translations, yet this word makes the statement so comprehensive – why should something at all be and not purely nothing.

[177] E. Coreth, Metaphysics, 121.

[178] Cf. Paul Edwards, ed. *Encyclopedia of Philosophy*, vol. 8 on Aquinas, p. 109. The co-extensivity of attributes of being with what is, is not exhausted in the reality of existence.

an overstatement to maintain that the facticity of existence is a *conditio sine qua non* for any other activity or for any pursuit and satisfaction of any value. No wonder traditional philosophy perceives 'existence' as a perfection in contradiction to non-existence considered to be an imperfection or defect.

To make the discussion more concrete, it is worthwhile that we recall here those four major classifications/types of value which were examined earlier (i.e., infra-human, infra human-moral, moral and religious values). As one can detect, all those four values are dependent on the *absolute ground* that *there exists* a human subject in the very first place. The human person exists in different circumstances, attending or attracted to some values. When he exists in one circumstance, merely responding to his in-born human desires, he attends to *infra-human values*. And when he exists in another moment where he is faced with making moral decision in the face of several options, he responds to a *moral value*. Yet, before he can attend to any value at all, he must exist in the first place. Hence, the famous saying: *"Primum vivere deinde philosophare"*.

Confronting the foregoing discourse with the Nigerian society which this paper obliges itself to make an occasional reference, one quickly sees a society that is imperceptibly exterminating itself as long as it promotes an environment that encourages the shedding of blood and all kinds of dehumanization like kidnapping, suicide, human rituals, human trafficking, Fulani herdsmen's menace, etc. In these unpleasant acts that dehumanize the person, the primordiality of life is both debased and trivialized.

**(b) The Primordiality of Truth-Objectivity Yielding to Justice/Peace**
Like in the preceding discussion on existence, the question of truth and objectivity is acknowledged to have been at the foundations of most human activities in any progressive society. It is important to note that the discussion here is more existential than theoretical, meaning that the concern of this paper on truth-objectivity does not border on theories of truth or epistemic discourse on issues of objectivity versus subjectivity. Even when occasional references are made to the theoretical grounding of the discussions, the focus shall be to explain truth-objectivity on the plane of human interaction, and how the duo

brings about fairness (justice) and enthrones peace – values that cannot be automatically bought by money (economic value) or acquired through the magical performance of religious rituals. Though religion, when properly lived, can open one up to appreciate truth, leading to peace/harmony, but religious activities are being flawed today by insincerity and subjectivity instead of objectivity/truth.

To begin the discussion of this section, it might be nice to refer again to Aristotle for a support. For him, truth is a very fundamental value; a value that is tied with human nature and so with human existence itself. In his *Metaphysics*, Aristotle maintains that everyone possesses an aspect of the truth, not completely but partially: "…no one is able to attain the truth adequately, while, on the other hand, no one fails entirely, but *everyone says something true about the nature of things…*" [179] By this statement, Aristotle implies that nobody has a monopoly of the truth; rather, truth is a natural endowment of everybody. This being the case, truth therefore transcends any person, or race or class of persons or authority. It is in this *universal trait* of truth that we see its transcendence. Someone can immediately pose the question – Why then do people err if everyone has some aspects of the truth? From Aristotle, we learn that the truth that each person possesses is only a part. Another way of understanding that is to argue that all humans have the potentiality to open up to the truth of things at any time, and whenever a person errs, it is only because he refuses to open himself to the illumining light of the truth, preferring the blockade which ignorance and passions of various kinds offer him. For this reason, truth always goes with objectivity – which is knowledge that is certain and public, not subjective and personal. It is to guarantee such knowledge that Aristotle defines philosophy as the pursuit of truth: "…philosophy should be called **science or knowledge of truth**. For the end of theoretical knowledge is truth, while that of practical knowledge is action."[180] If we accept the validity of the ancient dictum that *agere sequitur esse*, and if part of the constitution of our *esse* is the knowledge we have (including the 'knowledge of truth'), then the value called

---

[179] Cf. Aristotle, Metaphysics, Book Alpha the less, no. 993a-b. The opening sentence.

[180] Ibid., 993b.

'truth' is connected to human existence. In this way, truth like existence itself, remains a primordial value.

Even among the schoolmen, notably in Aquinas, we see a heightened emphasis on the fundamentality of truth when, in discussing the transcendental attribute of the true, Aquinas makes truth the reason for the intelligibility of anything at all. That is to say that we are driven to desire to knowledge only because there is some truth to be discovered and which, as it were, draws us to itself. Kreyche articulates the point as follows: "Because *things are said to be true*, they are intelligible, and because they are intelligible, they are such that *they can be known*."[181] Some of the philosophers anchored the truth on a person – a divine person of course. For instance, Berkeley had vehemently criticized the doctrines of abstraction and materialism because they try to contradict the truth, whereas for him, philosophy is defined as *"nothing else but the study of wisdom and truth"*.[182] And the truth about things is that whatever is known is known in the form of ideas, not as a piece of matter outside the mind, but as ideas within the mind. The outcome of this reasoning is this: "whatever exists, exists only because it is perceived by a mind": *esse est percipi aux percipere*. However, the perception is not necessarily by a human mind, but by a divine mind: God acts on the spirits or minds to create a "material world" [the perceived world for human], and truly speaking, humans do not see the things in God, but rather, and borrowing from the scriptures, he says, "we live, more and exist in God".[183] Here then, both existence and truth are united in a divine mind. Also, Spinoza has found absolute truth/objectivity in a divine being. He criticized the famous Descartes "I think" philosophy on what he saw as two inadequacies that rendered the expression a useless statement. The first inadequacy is that it is a "merely contingent truth" whereas certainty must be founded on necessities. The second inadequacy is that the expression contains an inalienable reference to a first person whereas access to philosophical truth [otherwise called truth

---

[181] R. J. Kreyche, First Philosophy: An Introductory Text in Metaphysics, p. 188.

[182] George Berkeley, *Principles of Human Knowledge and Three Dialogues* ed, by R. Woolhouse (London: Penguin Books, 1988), 37. § or no. 1.

[183] Julian Marias., *History of Philosophy*, transl. by Stanley Appelbaum & C. G, Strowbridge, (NY: Dover Pub. Inc, 1967), 257.

that is certain] comes "when we rise above preoccupation with our own limited experience… and learn to see things from the impartial point of view of the rational observer to whom things appear 'under the aspect of eternity' (*sub species aeternitatis*)."[184] Even Leibniz does have a similar view, when criticizing Locke, he opines that all truths do not depend on experience, but some are innate as they contain necessary truths which are, as it were, imprint in us, and which we only discover by what he calls 'means of attention'.

To understand the question of truth in the above trend of thought is to understand its primacy among many things. This being the case, our encounter with the truth raises several consequences. The first is that we do not pretend to have acquired the truth or to have taken a position to legislate over it. In the words of Karl Jaspers, our encounter with the truth is one of a continuous search; of someone who is "perpetually on the way toward its discovery'. Such attitude is the task of philosophy, observes Jaspers."[185] A second consequence comes from Josef Pieper's observation with regard to the intricate connection between language, truth and communication. Firstly, and leaning on Plato, he argues that words accomplish a two-fold purpose, namely, they convey reality: "we speak in order to name and identify something that is real, to identify it for someone" – a point that connects to its second purpose, viz, that "human speech/language has an interpersonal character." The second consequence of understanding truth existentially can be articulated thus: when anyone is not guided by the intention 'to convey reality' (to convey the true) as he is using words, that person *ceases from communication because he no longer considers his partner as a person, an equal,* "because he does not respect him as a human subject, but now takes him as an object to toil with."[186] This is the error of flattery and lies. Rather than being acts of communication of a type, flattery and lies are rather blockades in communication process.

---

[184] Cf. Roger Scruton, *A Short History of Modern Philosophy: From Descartes to Wittgenstein* (London: Routledge, 1991), 51.

[185] Karl Jaspers, *Way to Wisdom* (New Haven and London: Yale University Press, 1954), 12.

[186] Josel Pieper, *Abuse of Language, Abuse of Power,* (San Francisco, Ignatius Press, 1988), 16.

Bringing the foregoing primacy of truth into the Nigerian state, it is a common knowledge that our Nigerian governments, from the military era till date (2019), have been increasingly enlarging their quantity of advisors who, unfortunately, see their primary assignment as supporters of the government of the day through flattery and lies to the citizens. Examples abound everywhere. More unfortunately is that such untruths and deception have also crept into many Christian Churches whose pastors and priests imperceptibly manipulate their worshippers to their financial desires. In these circumstances, truth as a primordial value is speedily vanishing from our society.

## (c) The Primordiality of Human Freedom and Responsibility

One of the best expressions that depict the fundamental nature of human freedom is the coinage of Jean Jacque Rousseau thus: "man was born free, and he is everywhere in chains. Those who think themselves masters of others are indeed greater slaves than they".[187] Given that no antecedent premise led Rousseau to this affirmation, his position may appear axiomatic from where elucidations are later made. Of course, there could be a possible debate on how one's birth into a family and in a particular country that is not chosen by him could be said to have been born free. It seems that there is a general acceptance that a child has freedom as an inalienable right as soon as he is born. It is a freedom that derives from the fact that none of us can choose the other's birth for him. Not even a child's parent. They cannot be said to have chosen and determined the entire infant life of the child, and in this way, we can see how freely every child is born. Such inalienable right of birth is enshrined in most constitutions of various nations and heightened by United Nations Charter of 1948.[188] But as a point of departure, it must be asked 'what actually does human freedom mean?' This question is a complex one, especially when it is considered alongside its opposite, determinism. However, the scope of our consideration here is one of isolating some central elements that depict freedom as a transcendent primordial value.

---

[187] Jean Jacque Rousseau, The Social Contract, ch. 1 – the opening sentence.

[188] See Art. No. 1 which states: "All human beings are born free and equal in dignity and rights. They are endowed with reason and conscience and should act toward one another in a spirit of brotherhood".

Generally considered, freedom is defined as '*the absence of coercion or constraint*'. In other words, someone is free to the degree that he can choose from among options that are available to him without being constrained from choosing the way he wants or without being coerced to choose in a particular way.[189] Freedom understood in this way is called **negative freedom** since it refers to **"freedom from"**.

Furthermore, some thinkers have argued that it is not enough that there be absence of coercion by another person, but also that *there be no natural condition* which may impose obstructions and restraints on the human capacity to choose from the available alternatives.

There is *another dimension* to the concept of freedom: it concerns the means or power to achieve what one is choosing or desiring.

For those who include this dimension to the concept of freedom, there would be three necessary conditions upon which freedom is guaranteed, namely:

> a. That there be absence of coercion
>
> b. That there be no obstruction by natural condition and
>
> c. That there be available means or power to achieve the objective of one's choice.[190]

It is equally argued for that there is *need to understand coercion not only in terms of prohibitions or commands, but also in terms of all forms of twisting of facts* like manipulation, deception and even the denial of information/knowledge that might be helpful to someone who is making a choice to do so freely and correctly.[191] Where such indirect forms of restraint exist, we do not speak of true freedom. Again, we can speak of **freedom in the positive sense**. When there is a claim of freedom

---

[189] Cf. Partridge, "Freedom" in Paul Edward, ed., The Encyclopedia of Philosophy, vol. 3, p. 222.

[190] Ibid., 222.

[191] Ibid., 222.

for oneself, this claim bespeaks of not only absence of coercion, but also that of which freedom is claimed. In political or social freedom, a claim for freedom is not only with reference to being released from a certain constraint, but also the ability to exercise that for which freedom is claimed. For instance, *the right and freedom to vote and be voted for in a socio-political structure does not only show absence of coercion, but more the dignity of belonging and insertion into one's society.*

With regard to kinds of freedom, the following classification can be made:

a. *Physical Freedom*: This kind of freedom refers to the absence of any physical constraint or physical coercion. An example could be given with someone who is released from prison; he is no longer confined within the physical walls of the prison. Such regained right can also be called political freedom with regard to the earlier example given about the right to vote that may have been denied a political prisoner.

b. *Moral Freedom*: this is the absence of moral restraint or absence of a moral duty/obligation.

c. *Religious Freedom*: the kind that refers to one's liberty to choose and practice any faith of one's choice.

d. *Psychological Freedom*: this refers to the liberty to control oneself in the midst of natural appetites, emotions and instincts. This capacity of control distinguishes human beings from lower animals which are generally ruled by instincts. For instance, a goat will have an unrestrained desire to eat any yam tuber within its vicinity no matter how many times one chases it away from the scene.

e. *Abstract Freedom*: this kind of freedom is rather a loose coinage that refers to a number of many things like freedom of expression, freedom of assembly, freedom of movement, etc.

At this stage, it is pertinent to underline a particularly important factor in the concept of freedom, namely, ***the centrality of liberty/choice.*** This element is the thrust of the thesis of freedom. Some philosophers or social writers opine that we can speak truly of freedom if one can choose *deliberately* and with *initiative* and *responsibility*. John Stuart Mill's work *On Liberty* is a good exposition of this way of thinking. In chapter three of this work, he makes an interesting argument on the question of individuality (i.e., the freedom of the individual person) which, according to him, brings about "well-developed human beings", thereby fostering the development of the society. Such development comes about via the spirit of originality which individuality promotes. And it is original thinking and practice, championed usually by a few that have ever brought progress to the society. Hence, he considers any 'democratic government' and 'numerous aristocracy' as government of mediocrity because of an inbuilt logic of mass in them. Given what he calls "tyranny of opinion", eccentricity is not only a reproach, but it is desirable'. It seems that one of his best expressions of the thesis of individuality lies in this statement:

> There is no reason that all human existence should be constructed on some one or some small number of patterns. If a person possesses any tolerable amount of common sense and experience, his own mode of laying out his existence is the best, not because it is the best in itself; but because it is his own mode. Human beings are not like sheep; and even sheep are not undistinguishably alike.[192]

Much as some difficulties are latent in this view of Mill, the point in citing him is to stress the fact of an individual initiating his action deliberately and being allowed to do so too.

Even before Mill, the medieval thinker St. Augustine had a work titled *De Liberio Arbitrio Voluntatis* i.e., *On the Free Choice of the Will* where he argues first of all that "God created man freely, endowing him from the beginning an autonomy like his soul as his counsel which

---

[192] John Stuart Mill, On Liberty, Chapter Three or See: Mary Warnock, Utilitarianism and On Liberty, Including Mill's 'Essay on Bentham' and Selections from the Writings of Jeremy Bentham and John Austin (London: Blackwell Publishing, 2003), 141.

he uses voluntarily and not coerced…".[193] Furthering his argument, especially against Manichaeism, he maintains that because of the reason that man is endowed with, he has the power to choose from diverse particular goods and hence of choosing an apparent good like selfish utility, illegitimate money, etc.[194] Many medieval thinkers followed the same trend that the will is free to choose in whichever direction it judges.

Furthermore, the *theory of agency* improves the explanation about the question of freedom and liberty. The theory maintains that 'a free and rational agent is a self-determining being', meaning that such a being can, as Taylor explains, be considered the cause of its own behaviour.[195]

According to Taylor, *when I believe that I have done something, I believe that it was I who did it and not just one of my inner states which is not identical with my entire self. Conversely, when I don't believe that I did something, it means that I don't believe that something identical with myself did it.* For instance, my pulse is caused and regulated by certain organic conditions existing within me of which I have no control. *The organic operation of my body cannot be regarded as my action because it is nothing but a "mechanical reflex"*, borrowing Taylor's words.

Given the foregoing situation, the *theory of agency* requires the postulation of *two metaphysical notions:* Firstly, the theory '*postulates that there must be the notion of a self or a person*' who is not a mere bundle of perceptions in the description of the human mind by David Hume, but "a substance" and "a self-moving substance".

Secondly, this self-determining substance becomes the cause of its action, and would not be referring to antecedent conditions. What this amounts to is that *"an agent is sometimes a cause, without being an antecedent sufficient condition."[196]* A self-determining agent as causing his action can validly be spoken of when we mean an agent that originates an act with initiative and performs it to a considerable extent.

---

[193] Cf. Paolo Valori, Il Libero Arbitrio: Dio, L'uomo, La Libertà (Milano: Rizzoli Libri, 1987), 30.

[194] Ibid. p. 31. My translation from the Italian original.

[195] Cf. Taylor, Metaphysics, p. 50.

[196] Ibid., p. 51.

The foregoing reflection on human freedom that is linked with responsibility has a lot to criticize about our Nigerian society where the following scenario is prevalent:

- A politician comes out to contest election, wins it amid all controversies, fails to perform, but he is bold to give himself excuses as he blames his predecessors. In this way, he ignores completely his responsibility.

- A student fails examination, but rather than finding out where he got it wrong, he is quick to conclude that he was failed by his teacher who never liked him.

- Many self-styled and orthodox pastors/priests try to intimidate their congregations to donate monies of their expectations, using the name of God, and yet, preaching to them that they are free children of God.

- A sizeable number of civil servants take glory only in either maintaining the status-quo in their places of work or worse still, lowering the standard that they met, but generally claim that government budgeting is so poor even as they do not show the least creativity and plans.

**Finding Solution in the Education of the Human Personality**

First of all, it is important to ask the question – what is education in general and what does it entail? To answer this question, it has to be noted that education has a controversial origin. It is controversial in the sense that there are two prominent origins of the word; origins that bespeak of two traditions and meanings. While a first tradition maintains that the word "education" derives from a Latin verb – *"educare"* which means "to train" or "to form", the second tradition holds that the word came from a cognate verb – "educere" meaning "to lead out". [197] These two traditions represent what has come to be called the formalist and naturalist theories of education. Those who consider

---

[197] Cf. Augustine Odinkalu, "The End of Education", The Torch Magazine, Dec. 2003-2004, (Enugu: .......), 64.

education to be a way of training individuals into becoming certain or particular personalities belong to the formalist group whereas those who perceive education as a leading-out are the naturalists i.e., they think that every individual is capable of developing on its own, having been endowed with an inner capacity for such development. The group would have Plato as a reputable reference-point because Plato had maintained that virtue like knowledge cannot be taught; they are acquired through divine dispensation via the act of recollection.[198]

All said and done, there is a way that the two traditions on the origin of the concept of education can be united. It does not seem that the molding of a person's physical, moral, social and intellectual dimensions of his life can come all from external sources alone just as they cannot all come from the individual alone. The mature personality with good balance of those dimensions is rather a mixture of the two sources: the external and the internal factors.

Beyond the etymological meanings of the term "education", there have been notable philosophers who contributed a lot to education. We shall only mention two of such personalities, not because their views exhaust all other views, but because they have good elements that form basis for our proposal here. One of the philosophers in mind here is **John Dewey** whose view on education underlines the aforesaid combination of formalist and naturalist theories. In Dewey's view, "the purpose of education should not revolve around the acquisition of a pre-determined set of skills, but rather the realization of one's full potential and the ability to use those skills for the greater good."[199] According to him, particularly as espoused in his work *My Pedagogic Creed*, Dewey thinks that preparing the students for future life means to assist them to have a mastery of themselves so that they can properly make use of their potentials. He also has another work, captioned *The Child and the Curriculum*, where he "discusses two major conflicting schools of thought regarding educational pedagogy". With regard to the first school, the emphasis is on the curriculum and its contents. By this is meant, the subjects that are to be taught and the manner of teaching them. Such pedagogy, according to him, produces immature and

---

[198] Plato, Meno, 71a – 99b.

[199] Cf. Dewey on "Education and Teacher Education", Wikipedia.

dependent students as it perceives the students as subjects to be filled with knowledge. But there is also a second school, namely, child/student-centredness. For Dewey, there could be excesses, were every education to be left on the hands of the individual person. All the same, it is his contention that in the second school of thought, "we must take our stand with the child and our departure from him. It is he and not the subject-matter which determines both quality and quantity of learning".[200]

Contributing to the meaning and aims of education, **Bertrand Russell**, first of all, defines education as "the key to the rearing up of a new man of excellence".[201] Speaking about excellence, one imagines that Russell must have thought of the Greek origin of the word "excellence" – which is "arête" and means the same thing as virtue such that an educated man can be termed a virtuous man; a man of integrity. How education can produce a man of excellence is shown in Russell's four tasks/goals of education, namely, vitality, courage, sensitiveness and intelligence.[202] By *vitality* is meant the ability of educational process to promote an individual's good health and hence hard work, avoiding boredom and all that can make him feel envious of others' successes. Also education should aim at molding a *courageous personality*, one who is ready to confront fear-arousing events. With *sensitiveness* as another aim to be pursued in education, Russell means the effort to instill in someone a good control of himself, especially in his emotions, passions and expressions while paying particular attention to the feelings and conditions of others, conditions that involve pleasure and pain. On the fourth aim which is *intelligence*, Russell explains it to display two fronts: 'actual knowledge' and 'received knowledge. But his notion of intelligence in this context bespeaks of the tendency and process of acquiring knowledge rather than knowledge already acquired.

---

[200] Ibid, See also: Dewey, The Child and the Curriculum, 1902, pp. 13-14.

[201] Bertrand Russel, *On Education, Especially in Early Childhood* (London: Unwin Hyman, 1926), 41.

[202] Bertrand Russell, *On Education, Especially in Early Childhood* (London: Unwin Hyman Ltd, 1926), 41.

Looking at the elements that are basic in the views of the two philosophers of education X-rayed above, it is obvious that the mature development of the individual is the key – a development that is not the learning of creeds, but a system of learning that opens the individual to personally perceive, discuss, analyze and project ideals that are helpful to him and the society.

In the light of the foregoing, this paper proposes an end to "paper/certificate education" and a strong pursuit of cognitive and volitional education. The former is a continuous effort to know and to be able to rationally sort out values in the descending order of primordiality; the latter is the praxis of acting in accordance with the hierarchically arranged values. For nothing gets done, except by actually doing it. The act of doing is primarily the movement of the will – voluntas – and hence, the education and re-education of the will must complement the knowledge of values.

# Chapter 9

# The Centralized Federalism in Nigerian Political Structure: A Critical Analysis for Decentralization

Eugene C. Anowai
And
Steven Chukwujekwu

## Abstract

*Nigeria is a multiethnic, multinational, multi-religious, multicultural country characterized by deep-rooted ethnic diversities and political heterogeneities. It began to adopt a federal system from October 1954; about forty years after the British colonial masters through the process of forced Amalgamation that brought the nationalists together without the consent of the constituent bodies in flagrant disregard of the sharp disparities and the wish of the people. However, the politicians constitutionally instituted a federal system to properly accommodate the heterogeneities and pluralities among the regions. The federal system has been in operation since then. But this federal system is not working and creates complex challenges, due to the diverse nature of Nigeria and the centralized nature of its federalism. Therefore, it is opined that for it to work properly as a true federation, it is imperative that it has to be decentralized. So rather than 'one size fits all' nature of Nigerian federalism, this paper argues that devolved government bodies will tailor public services and regulations more efficiently and flexibly to meet the needs of each particular region. Consequently, this paper discusses the contradictory impulses toward true federalism in Nigeria. After discussing the analytical issues related to the specific nature of decentralization in federal systems, and taking into consideration the conventional academic and political wisdom, it sustains that decentralization of Nigerian federalism is urgent and imperative if it would be sustained.*

*Keywords: diversity, heterogeneity, Amalgamation, federalism, decentralized federalism, centralized federalism*

## Introduction

The dissolution of the multinational and multi-ethnic empires like the Russian, the Ottoman and the Austro-Hungarian, and the defeat of the Kaiser Reich, led to the emergence of nation-states that enjoyed neither religious, nor linguistic, nor cultural homogeneity. The states that result out of this dissolution like Poland, Austria, Hungary, Czechoslovakia, Bulgaria, Yugoslavia, Lithuania, Latvia, Estonia, the Greek and the Turkish republics, have territories in which large numbers of national minorities reside. Also, the scramble for, the colonization and partition of Africa resulted in the many countries with the conglomeration of many ethnic and national minorities living together. A case in point is Nigeria, a multi-ethnic, multireligious, multilingual and multicultural nation. As it is today, because of global political situation, most countries are culturally diverse.

In Nigeria, the 1966 termination of the extant federalism of the first republic gave rise to a series of events that eventually culminated in the present trivialisation federalism – consisting of thirty-six nominal and dependent states which are inevitably subservient to a patronising and hegemonic central government.

The recent political events in Nigeria suggest that majority of her citizens are progressively demanding for True Federalism and Restructuring; the situation which can be described as a flooding river under an unstoppable rain. As political philosopher Thomas Hobbes famously wrote, "The ever-looming sense of war is similar to an inclination to rain; actual fighting". The Nigerian experience shows that every day, there are tendencies toward violence that could suddenly erupt like a sudden rain shower.

That is why there is urgent need for decentralisation of our highly centralised federal government which I regard as an aberration of modern politics of multi-nationalism. At this juncture there is a need for us to take a short historical journey to understand the philosophy behind the amalgamation of Nigeria by British colonial Lords despite her diversities and heterogeneities.

## A Short Historical Journey to the Origin of Nigeria

Nigeria is a multiethnic and multilingual country. Hansfort et al. (1976) reported that there are 394 different languages and many ethnic groups. From a historical point of view, Nigeria is a multilingual, multiethnic, multinational polity brought together as a geopolitical unity by the British colonial power in 1914 (Nigerian amalgamation) and this will enable us to see whether its existence as a united and indivisible entity is a settled matter, as some people among the democratic citizens of Nigeria assert.

On 1st January 1914, Laggard delivered the "Amalgamation Speech". He announced to the whole world the basis on which this is to be carried out. The basis in my calculation was of course to facilitate the continued systematic exploitation of the people and their resources. I quote it verbatim:

> *His majesty the king has decided that from today (1st Jan. 1914, 9am) all the country from the sea to near the desert in the north, and from the French country in the west to the German Cameroons in the East, shall be one single country under Governor-General, so that there may be no jealousy or rivalry between the North and the South, and all may co-operate together for the advancement of peace and prosperity. His majesty has been pleased to appoint me, Sir. F. Laggard, as Governor-General, and by the help of God I trust that I may be able to obtain wisdom to discharge this responsible task worthily. It will be my earnest endeavour to promote peace and justice for all men, to protect everyman in the observance of his own religious faith, and to administer equal justice alike for great and small.*
>
> *There will also be a council for Nigeria upon which the Europeans holding highest offices in Nigeria will have seats and also natives representing each part of Nigeria. These will be nominated by me. There will also be an executive council consisting of the principal officers of the administration to assist the Governor-General with their advice. There will be one Supreme Court for Nigeria, and Sir Edwin Speed is appointed Chief Justice of Nigeria. I trust that under the new*

> *method of Government Nigeria will increase in prosperity
> and wealth, and its people in happiness.*[203]

So, by this promulgation, Lord Laggard amalgamated the northern and southern territories in the name of British Crown, setting the borders of what becomes Nigeria, a name coined sixteen years before by Laggard's future wife, Flora Shaw, in an article she wrote for the British establishment newspaper *The Times*. A German Karl Maier, in his book *This House Has Fallen: Nigeria in Crisis*, observed that "the joining was not for the purposes of nation building. The simple reason was that the North's colonial budget was running at a deficit and only link with the profitable south could eliminate the needed British subsidy".[204]

Laggard made the audacious decision to merge what was the Northern part of Niger area with the southern part to create Nigeria. Before then, the two regions lived distinct and separate not having much in common. But he felt it was expedient to create the new country Nigeria purely for administrative convenience. No account was taken of the differences in culture, tradition, religion and for that matter the wish of the people being submerged. They are colonial subjects and so left for the master to do as he pleased. Hence, it was not negotiated and entered into by various nationalities that make up the country. No one was consulted to discuss and consent to live together.

No wonder a prominent Northern Nigerian, Abubakar Tafawa Balewa, who was destined to become the first federal prime minister, in 1948 made a point that is worth mentioning here. He remarked that "since 1914, the British Government has been trying to make Nigeria into one country, but the Nigerian people themselves are historically different in their backgrounds, in their religious beliefs and customs and do not show themselves any signs of willingness to unite. Nigerian unity is only British invention".[205]

---

[203] Verbatim report of Sir F. Lugard's inaugural speech as Nigerian Amalgamator and Governor General. (Administration and progress in Nigeria 1914).

[204] Maier K, *This House Has Fallen: Nigeria in Crisis*, (Penguin Books, 2002), 10.

[205] Meredith M., *The State of Africa: A History of Fifty Years of Independence*, (Free Press, New York, 2006), p. 8.

Adisa Adeleye alluded to this statement when he said, "it is a pity that it was in Northern Nigeria that the question of the amalgamation of the 1914 was raised in the 1950s". The late Prime Minister of Nigeria, Sir Alhaji Abubakar Tafawa Balewa was reported in 1952 in a speech in the Northern House of Assembly, Kaduna, that:

> *The Southern people who are swarming into this region daily in large numbers are really intruders. We don't want them and they are not welcome here in the North.*
>
> *Since the amalgamation in 1914, the British Government has been trying to make Nigeria into one country, but the Nigerian people are different in every way including religion, custom, language and aspiration. The fact that we're all Africans might have misguided the British Government. We here in the North, take it that `Nigerian unity` is not for us.[206]*

The McPherson Constitution which brought the different parts of Nigeria into political discourse also portrayed the fragile nature of the political entity of the country. After the alleged maltreatments of Northern legislators in 1953 on Independence motion by the late Chief Anthony Enahoro of the West, the Sardauna of Sokoto and the leader of the Northern People's Congress (NPC) was quoted as saying, 'the mistake of 1914 has come to light'.[207] He elaborated further that, 'Lord Lugard and the amalgamation were far from popular among us at that time. There were agitations in favour of successions; we should set up on our own. We should cease to have any more to do with the Southern people. We should take our own way'.[208]

In a book published in 1947, the Yoruba leader Obafemi Awolowo, who dominated western Nigerian politics for more than thirty years, wrote: "Nigeria is not a nation. It is a mere geographical expression. There are no 'Nigerians' in the same sense as there are 'English', Welsh', or 'French'. The word Nigeria is merely a distinctive

---

[206] Adeleye A, "Amalgamation of 1914: Was it a Mistake?"

[207] Adeleye A,

[208] Adeleye A,

appellation to distinguish those who live within the boundaries of Nigeria and those who do not".[209]

Also, Dim Odumegwu Ojukwu with an incredible vibrancy aptly remarked in *The Ahiara Declaration*:

*The federation of Nigeria is today as corrupt as unprogressive, as oppressive and irreformable as Ottoman Empire was in Eastern Europe over a century ago. And in contrast, the Nigerian federation in form it was constituted by the British cannot by any stretch of imagination be considered an African necessity. Yet we are being forced to sacrifice our very existence as a people to the integrity of that ramshackle creation that has no justification either in history or in the freely expressed wishes of the people. Nigeria was made up of peoples and groups with very little in common.[210]*

While some might see this as raising unnecessary alarm but his characterization of the country fifty three years ago rings true today. In Nigeria, secessionist threats or separatist agitations have been attributable to a number of factors: the country's heterogeneous ethnic composition, cultural diversity, vast size, inept administrative practices, and controversial political and constitutional arrangements, personality clashes between Nigerian leaders before and after independence. These issues do not constitute authentic ingredients of proper amalgamation. So, the way Nigeria was formed as a nation will continue to raise issues that militate against the unity and centrality of Nigeria federalism. In my candid opinion, the agitations would continue to surface and resurface until the contentious issues are given the attention they deserve. And according to a political scientist A. Appadorai, "unless some political units desire to unite and establish their common interests, there is no basis for federation".[211]

---

[209] Meredith M., *The State of Africa, A History of Fifty Years of Independence*, p. 8.

[210] Ojukwu Odumegwu C, *The Ahiara Declaration: The Principles of the Biafran Revolution*, (Mark Press Switzerland, 1969), 10-11.

[211] Appadorai A, *The Substance of Politics*, (Oxford Uni Press, 1975) 498.

140

**Nigerian Federal System**

Federalism, loosely defined, means that there is a meaningful distinction between the Central Government and locally-devolved governing bodies, either States, Provinces, Districts, Counties or Autonomous Regions. Basically, beyond that, anything applies, including some, or all, of the following characteristics:

1. That there is a balance of political and governmental power shared (in whatever relative proportion) between local governments and the Central (or Federal) Government.

2. That devolved political regions and bodies essentially handle their own affairs, usually entrusting major portfolios such as foreign affairs and defense to the Federal Government.

3. That the Federal Government and the devolved political bodies are legally distinct entities representing the same country (in terms of international affairs).

4. And, most controversially, that the devolved political bodies are accorded the protection from excessive Federal interference where none is due (also known in The United States).

Many countries have adopted Federal systems, especially so when a new nation is being carved out of several culturally and ethno-linguistically diverse regions; each with their own political interests and concerns. A prime example of federalism would be India, where the only way a united nation-state could survive was through a carefully-crafted federal system that would preserve the territorial and political integrity of the nation-state while not descending into undemocratic tyranny.

But in the case of Nigeria, the constitution grants the central government strong formal powers over an extensive list of functions, including over civil and criminal law, state and federal elections, finance, trade and commerce, taxation, education, health and social security, with federal law taking precedence over state laws. All serve to rubber-stamp the centralized government's policies. As all major taxing powers reside with the central government, state and local authorities rely for their revenues upon transfers. Professor Soludo Charles captured this point vividly when he remarked in his independence lecture that:

> *The tax system was also largely centralized. Today, if State x labours hard to attract companies to its state or even builds industries, the corporate tax revenues would be paid into the Federation Account and shared to everyone. Similarly, if a state promotes tourism, all the VAT collected (including from alcohol and cigarettes) would be paid into the Federation Account and shared to all – including states where alcohol and cigarettes are banned.[212]*

This is a despotic central government system; absorbing other powers and menacing the private liberties of the citizens and having large mass of functions which virtually proves too heavy. A clearer example of Nigerian federalism is that obtained during the period of Communist control in the USSR, where power was highly centralized.

Akin Osuntokun offers us much food for thought when he said:

> So, if what we practise in Nigeria is not federalism and we insist on calling it federalism then it is correct to call it by its proper name and that is false federalism. It is this false identification that gives validity to the notion of true federalism. As in the tradition of dialectical materialism, every tendency presupposes its contradiction and to every thesis there is the antithesis.[213]

Necessity they say is a mother of invention. "The current Nigerian constitution, which entrenches a centralised, top-down, unitary federalism or what a commentator has aptly described as feeding bottle federalism is

---

[212] Soludo C. "Restructuring Nigeria for Prosperity" in *The Politics of Biafra and the Future of Nigeria*, (Safari Books, Ibadan, 2016), 250.

[213] Akin Osuntokun, "What is True Federalism?" This Day online, August 5, 2016 1:25.

a system that Nigeria as a pluralist nation does not need".[214] Therefore, common sense suggests that we must look for an alternative. The alternative is that we must redesign the Nigerian federation for productivity and prosperity. We redesign it by decentralization and devolution of power in our federal system. So that the powers of the regions that were eroded and transferred to federal authority should be reversed.

As it is today, because of global political situation, most countries are culturally diverse. The world democracies are becoming more complex and increasingly multi-cultural and multi-national. According to recent estimate, the world's 184 independent states contain over 600 living language groups, and 5,000 ethnic groups. In very few countries, can the citizens be said to share the same language or belong to the same ethno-national group. And this is the greatest challenge facing democracy today especially in Nigeria. Bearing this in mind, we can see how the position of the Igbo Nation at the National Conference for a renegotiated Constitution for Nigeria appropriate solution is in addressing governance issues in our multinational federated country. The position on Federalism states: In a true Federalism, the powers of central Government should be narrowly circumscribed, and whittled down to issues that affect the entire country, such as Defence (external and internal), Foreign Affairs, Immigration, Monetary and Fiscal Policy, Customs and Excise and the settings of standard in other areas.[215] In effect, the position is that true federalism should be decentralised if not it is false and should not be referred as federalism.

## Decentralized Federal Constitutions

A decentralized federal system is characterized by fairly autonomous provinces and a weak central authority in the powers granted to the executive and national parliament. The Brazilian and American versions both exemplify cases with strong regional states and a relatively weak central government.

The process of devolution or decentralization is normally designed to secure a more efficient government. According to the world bank, decentralization means "the transfer of authority and responsibility for public functions from the central government to intermediate and local

---

[214] Soludo C, "Restructuring Nigeria for Prosperity," 247.

[215] "The Position of The Igbo Nation," At the National Conference for A Renegotiated Constitution for Nigeria, 2014, 12.

governments or quasi-independent government organizations and/or the private sector".[216] That is to say, Decentralization implies the existence of a central authority, a central government that can be decentralized according to the wishes of its democratic citizens.

Plural societies like Nigeria are characterized by the existence of multiple groups, whether demarcated by class, linguistic, religious, racial, tribal, or caste-based identities. Federalism and decentralization are thought to be particularly important strategies for plural societies where groups live in geographically concentrated communities and where the administrative boundaries for political units reflect the distribution of these groups. This arrangement allows spatially-concentrated groups a considerable degree of self-determination to manage their own affairs and to protect their own cultural, social, and economic interests within their own communities, for example to control religious teachings in school curriculums, to determine levels of local taxation and expenditure for poorer marginalized areas which have lost out to development, to administer internal security forces and justice systems, and to establish language policy regulating public broadcasting and official documents. Different institutional forms of decentralization, notably federal constitutions, have long been recommended as the preferred mode of democratic governance designed to maintain stability within multinational states.

Arend Lijphart theorizes that *if political boundaries for sub-national governments reflect social boundaries, diverse plural societies can become homogeneous within their regions, thereby reducing communal violence, promoting political stability, and facilitating the accommodation of diverse interests within the boundaries of a single state.*[217]

Lijphart is far from alone in emphasizing the importance of decentralization for stability, peace-building and democratic consolidation in fragile multinational states like Nigeria, Iraq and Sudan. Alfred Stephan is also a strong proponent of this form of government, suggesting that plural societies such as the Russian Federation, Indonesia, and Burma/Myanmar will never become consolidated democracies without workable federal systems. All stable

---

[216] The World Bank, 2002.

[217] Lijphart. *A, Patterns of Democracy.* (New Haven: Yale University Press, 1999). 196.

contemporary multinational democracies are federal, including Switzerland, Canada, Belgium, Spain and India.[218]

Nevertheless, decentralization is an elusive term. It has been used indistinctively to describe various degrees and forms of changing national government's role through:

> a) conveying decision-making capacity regarding policies and fiscal capacities to sub national authorities.
>
> b) transferring responsibilities for the implementation and administration of policies and programs defined at federal level to other spheres of government.
>
> c) shifting national government's attributions to the private or non-governmental sectors.

In other words, the term has been applied to processes of political and fiscal decentralization where functions and corresponding resources are transferred to sub-national spheres.

The coup of 1966 and the regime of Yakubu Gowon marked the start of the centralisation process. The process began with an attempt by his regime to create a centralised and unified Nigeria. Hence obsessed with the central goal of keeping Nigeria so united that no component part of it would ever be strong enough to threaten its unity, the military went ahead to literally dismantle most of the building blocks of federalism. The attempt was made to discard regional government and consolidate the different parts of Nigeria into thirty-six states through the process of forced inclusion and assimilation of the diverse peoples of the country. These powerful centralizing trends have been in operation since Yakubu Gowon's military regime propelled by different forces, responding to different motivations. But academic and political conventional wisdom, both within and outside Nigeria seems to say that this action is indeed wrong going by the composition of Nigeria (different ethnic, national, cultural and religious groups).

---

[218] Stephan. A, 'Federalism and Democracy: Beyond the US Model.' *Journal of Democracy*, 1999. 10(4): 19-34.

In point of fact, the concentration of fiscal resources at the federal level is a hallmark of bureaucratic authoritarianism in Nigerian federal system. Since this period, the widening of governmental action in the social domain has paralleled political centralization as well as the concentration of power at the Federal Executive.

Therefore, it was only too natural that democratic opposition to military rule took decentralization as one of its most cherished aims, together with social justice, rule of law, and citizens' participation. Decentralization to the local levels is argued for in the name of democracy as much as in the name of governmental efficiency and efficacy. It would supposedly allow for citizens' influence in decision-making, as well as for citizens' check over government actions.

Thus, there is no reason to think that decentralization inexorably implies the decrease in importance of the national government. It can result either in the creation of new fields for action, or in the definition of new, normative, regulative and re-distributive roles that coexist with the expansion of sub-national governments responsibilities. Decentralizing can take different forms like:

## Administrative Decentralization

Administrative decentralization transfers bureaucratic decision-making authority and managerial responsibilities for the delivery and regulation of public services and for raising revenues from the central government to sub-national tiers. This is the most basic form of decentralization. For example, where ministerial departments based in the national capital transfer administrative functions to provincial administrative bureaus and local field offices responsible for implementing central directives, regulating local areas, and running public health services, community planning, and schools.

## Fiscal Decentralization

This transfers some forms of resource allocation, usually by giving sub-national units authority over local taxes and spending. The prime emphasis has been to locate decisions about resources (revenues and expenditures) closest to the equivalent level of government. An extensive literature in political economy has examined the causes and consequences of fiscal decentralization and this process has been widely advocated as it is theorized to generate conditions most conducive to economic stability, allocative efficiency and distributive equity, thus maximizing social welfare.

## Political Decentralization

Political decentralization is a federal system which transfers authority and responsibility from the central government to public bodies at sub-national level, such as village assemblies, city mayors and state governors, and elected municipal councils. The prime motivation of political decentralization has been to strengthen opportunities for local control over public services and to expand opportunities for electoral accountability, political representation, and civil society engagement. The aim has been to give citizens, or their representatives, more voice in the formulation and implementation of local policies.

## The Principles of True Federalism and Nigerian Case

The relationship between federalism and decentralization, in conceptual and empirical terms, is far from being simple and uncontroversial.

In line with this thinking, Daniel Elazar points out that federations constitute non-centralized structures, emphasizing how they differ from decentralized states structures[219]: According to him, in its original form, as well as in its normative definition, federalism is characterized by non-centralization, i.e., by the diffusion of governmental powers among many centers, whose authority does not derive from the delegation of a central power, but is conferred by popular suffrage.

In the same vein, the Advisory Commission on Intergovernmental Relations 1981, remarks that North American federal model, simultaneously descriptive and prescriptive, in which "the powers of the general and state governments, even if they exist and are wielded within the same territorial limits, constitute distinct and separate sovereignties that act separately and independently, in their own spheres."[220] In Nigerian case, section 162 of 1999 Constitution of the Federal Republic of Nigeria states inter alia that:

---

[219] Elazar, Daniel. *Exploring Federalism*, (Alabama: University of Alabama Press, 1987).

[220] ACIR - Advisory Commission on Intergovernmental relations. 1981. The Condition of Contemporary Federalism: Conflicting Theories and Collapsing Constraints. Washington, 1981, 3.

*The Federation shall maintain a special account to be called the Federation Account into which shall be paid all revenues collected by the Government of the Federation... Any amount standing to the credit of the Federation Account shall be distributed among the Federal and State Governments and the Local government councils in each of the state on such terms and in such manner as may be prescribed by the National Assembly.[221]*

This portion of Nigerian Constitution shows how centralized its Federalism system is.

If one refers to the paragraph above, where I appointed that there were and are doubts about the unity of Nigeria, he will see immediately why there is a lack of trust. So due to lack of trust and suspicion, any sign of distinctiveness is widely seen as a threat and is often suppressed under the slogan: "One Nigeria". Can't we borrow a leaf from Ethiopia Federalism? In Ethiopia, the Constitution assigns mandates to the regional states (Article 52) as well as the federal government (Article 51), leaving the residual powers with the regional states (Article 52 (1)). Among other powers, the regional states enjoy cultural and linguistic autonomy. The mandates of the regional states are: ensuring self-government and the continuance of the democratic order based on the rule of law; exercising responsibility for socio-economic development policies; policing and public security on the state level; levying and collecting the regional taxes; and managing the regional civil service.

Following the structure of Ethiopia, Nigeria can make a paradigm shift. Instead of seeking unity through assimilation, unity can be achieved through the accommodation of diversities of all kinds, granting equal rights and status to all the groups in the country. The most important principles in this process have been the right to self-determination and equality of all regions. The rest of the world has been decentralising to achieve democracy and good governance. Presently, there are ongoing centralisation reforms in Bolivia, Ukraine, Pakistan and Zambia. Hence, if we want to compete economically and restore our reputation globally as a democracy, we must decentralise.

---

[221] Section 162, of 1999 of the Constitution of the Federal Government of Nigeria.

## The Gain of Decentralisation/True Federalism

From Montesquieu to Madison, philosophers and classical theorists suggest that decentralized governance has many advantages, especially:

(i) for democratic participation, representation, and accountability;

(ii) for public policy and governmental effectiveness; and

(iii) for the representation and accommodation of territorially based ethnic, cultural, and linguistic differences.

In particular, it is argued that the transfer of central decision-making to democratically elected local and regional bodies gives citizens multiple opportunities for meaningful development. Decentralization efforts are widely identified with the promotion of managerial efficiency and the enhancement of public services, as well as with more open, transparent, and accountable forms of representative democracy and the qualities of good governance. Trends toward decentralization crystallized in institutions will reshape the federal system as a complex cooperative arrangement in which regions expand their fiscal resources, competencies and responsibilities in providing social services.

## Resource Control as a Principle of True and Fiscal Federalism

Some of the geographically-largest and the most populous societies are federations including the United States, Canada, Germany, Brazil, India, and Russia. Hence about 41% of the world's population currently lives under this system of government. Federal constitutions are found in many global regions particularly in North America and Western Europe, although none are in Scandinavia and only one is found in the Middle East: the United Arab Emirates. All have system of resource control.

Professor Nwabueze, a constitutional lawyer, calls for philosophical and sober reflection on possible time bomb in Nigeria as things are falling apart and dropping in pieces due to our centralised federation when he refers to section 162(2) "that 'the principle of derivation shall be constantly reflected in any approved formula as being not less than 13 per cent of the revenue accruing to the Federation Account directly from any natural resources' runs counter to resource control as a principle of true and fiscal federalism".[222] He further delivers rich insights and outlines what should be regarded as the principles of true federalism:

- "Fiscal federalism requires that 'mines and minerals including oil fields, oil mining, geological surveys and natural gas' should be a residual matter within the exclusive competence of the regions or states.

- "Power with respect to these matters should, therefore, be expunged from the Exclusive Legislative List and be made a residual matter in accordance with the requirements of true and fiscal federalism.

- "Re-structuring, as it is presently being demanded, seeks to revert our federal system to the true federalism of the 1960/63 Constitutions, to further reduce the powers of the Federal Government as may be thought necessary, and to reverse the specific matters mentioned above."

As a matter of fact, current structure does not favour the majority of the citizens. The ethnic nationalities, other than those, in the meantime, in charge of the Federal Government, are groaning under the emasculating yoke of federal control, as evidenced by the recent authoritarian proscription of the present government.

In agreement with Professor Nwabueze, a chieftain of All Progressive Grand Alliance, APGA, in Abia State, Chief Prince Ukaegbu makes a striking case when he points out that the present structure of the Nigerian federation does not favour the masses and needs urgent restructuring. In an interview with *Vanguard* in Aba, Ukaegbu stated that the country will collapse if it is not restructured on the path of fiscal federalism to encourage production, competition and merit in the interest of the masses. He further establishes a critical point, remarks without mincing words that, "The current structure of

---

[222] "Why Nigeria must restructure —Nwabueze," On September 29, 2017, 12:32 am, In News by Urowayino WaramiCommen.

the Nigerian federation only favours the elite, leaving the masses to wallow in abject poverty. The elite are comfortable with the present state of affairs in this country, that is why some of them, particularly from the North, are against restructuring".[223] Nigeria is a rich nation with millions of poor masses. When you go to the Northern part of this country, the bulk of the people live in abject poverty with the elite in affluence. To an extent, it is the same situation in other sections of the country. As it is now, federal government wields political, economic and social powers to the disadvantage of the national groups. The general welfare, freedom, human right, self-development, and self-survival of the masses deteriorate progressively.

However, Restructuring and Devolution of powers will certainly not provide all the answers to our developmental challenges; but it will help to reposition our mindset as we generate new ideas and initiatives that would make our union worthwhile. The talk to have the country restructured means that Nigerians have agreed on our unity in diversity; that we should strengthen our structures to make the union more functional based on our comparative advantages.

## Recommendations

I submit that the current structure has urgent need for Restructuring. Therefore, this paper strongly advocates for devolution of powers to the extent that more responsibilities be given to the regions and states while the Nigerian Federal Government is vested with the responsibility to oversee areas like our foreign policy, and defense. That means we need to tinker with our constitution to accommodate new thoughts and ideas that will strengthen our nationality.

There is no serious doubt that huge numbers of people have beliefs and values that have been changed and shaped partly by challenges posed by contact with other cultures with other ways of seeing things. But common sense points to the fact that there is still the possibility for discussion. However, it must be noted that there is no easy solution because institutions once created assume life of their own with powerful interest groups that would do anything to ensure their continued

---

[223] "Decentralisation and Devolution of Power," On June 30, 2017, 5:57 am, In Vangard News Politics by Tony Comments by Emmanuel Aziken, Political Editor, Clifford Ndujihe, Dapo Akinrefon & Charles Kumolu.

existence. The politicians and current beneficiaries of the structure will not want any change to occur. But great men of wisdom admonished that reality is change. Ionic philosopher Heraclitus said that everything is in a state of perpetual change.

Hence I make the following recommendations, proposals and suggestions that can be put in place to effectively restructure and redesign Nigerian Federation:

1. Resort to dialogue as a means for amicable resolution of disagreements in a democracy. The democratic citizens must agree that based on experience that the current federalism does not and cannot work. Therefore, an urgent committee is needed to work out a constitution the reflects true federalism. How would decentralisation work in Nigerian setting as a pluralist Nation? How much power would be delegated to the federal government as opposed to the regions, this will form the core of the dialogue.

2. Introduce a decentralised political system in which six autonomous/semi-autonomous regions are formed, taking ethnicity partly into account. By that I mean, create regional governments mainly on the basis of 'ethnicity' and settlement patterns.

3. The six regions shall become federating units and operate largely on the principle of equity of regions in terms of representation and all spheres of national engagements.

4. Make more extensive powers exclusively assigned to the federal government. These include foreign affairs, national defence, financial and monetary policy, air, rail and water transport, inter-state commerce, patent and copy rights and nationality-related issues. The regional governments also have robust powers, apart from certain exclusive powers

such as ensuring the continuance of self-government and democratic order, entrusted with residual powers.

5. Grants each region "the right to a full measure of self-government, which includes the right to establish institutions of government in the territory that it inhabits and equitable representation in federal governments."

6. Nigeria should return to the revenue allocation formular in 1963 Republican Constitution. thereby stop the feeding bottle federalism. By that I mean, each region take charge of its mineral resources and pay taxes to the federal government. The federating units is to be fiscally viable entities because only then can they drive different economic transformation agenda.

7. The Nigerian decentralised governance system should now have five levels of government, i.e., federal, regional, state, and local governments.

## Conclusion

Democracy stimulates strong interests and ideas on decentralization. Decentralised governance system is not unfamiliar to Nigeria. Nigeria opposed military rule and we should consider decentralization as part and parcel of a new construction of a democratic polity. Furthermore, sub-national interests proved to be a powerful force during transition from authoritarianism to democratization. We should be all hands on deck in pursuing a crucial part in undermining the strong centralisation reminiscence of militarism, install true federalism: the political change we deserve in this challenging period. Therefore, after a critical analysis of the present structure I submit that the unity of Nigeria is feasible but a decentralisation and restructuring that will counter the inequalities and injustices that formed the base of her Federalism is a condition sine qua non.

May I conclude with the words of Prof. Chukwuma Solude in his independence day lecture on Restructuring Nigeria for prosperity:

> *I wish all Nigerians a happy independence! There is no better way to celebrate it than to ponder the dysfunctional structure of our federation and agree to re-engineer it. The powers of the various levels of government must be seriously reviewed. Abuja is too powerful to permit a competitive federalism.*[224]

---

[224] Soludo C, "Restructuring Nigeria for Prosperity," 262.